HEINEMANN HISTORY STUDY UNITS

THE REFORMATION

COLLE   HOUSE

HEINEMANN
EDUCATIONAL

Martyn Whittock

Heinemann Educational,
a division of Heinemann Educational Books Ltd,
Halley Court, Jordan Hill, Oxford OX2 8EJ

OXFORD LONDON EDINBURGH MADRID
ATHENS BOLOGNA PARIS MELBOURNE
SYDNEY AUCKLAND SINGAPORE TOKYO
IBADAN NÁIROBI HARARE GABORONE
PORTSMOUTH NH (USA)

First published 1992

British Library Cataloguing in Publication Data is available on request from the British Library.

ISBN 0–435–31280–4

Designed by Ron Kamen, Green Door Design Ltd, Basingstoke

Illustrated by Phil Burrows and Jeff Edwards

Printed in Hong Kong

The front cover shows *The St Bartholomew's Day Massacre* by François Dubois de'Amiens, an eyewitness to the event.

Icon information

Every Unit in this book includes the following symbol. When a section is filled in, it indicates the availability of extra resources included in the accompanying *Assessment and Resources Pack*.

Unit is referred to in an Extension Worksheet.

Unit is referred to in an Assessment Exercise.

For every Unit there is a Foundation Worksheet.

Acknowledgements

The author and publisher would like to thank the following for permission to reproduce photographs:

Ancient Art & Architecture Collection: 6.5D
Archiv für Kunst und Geschichte, Berlin: 3.2D, 3.2G
Bridgeman Art Library: 2.2B (Louvre); 3.1A (Church of St Marie, Wittenberg)
British Library: 7.1E
Bulloz: 6.2A
Mary Evans Picture Library: 2.3A
Gemäldegalerie, Staatliche Museen Preussischer Kulturbesitz, Berlin: 7.5A
Photographie Giraudon: 3.6A (Jurgens); 5.2E
Musée Cantonal des Beaux-Arts de Lausanne: cover, 7.3A
Museum of Fine Arts, Boston: 2.4A
Roger-Viollet: 4.2D
Scala: 1.2D, 2.5D, 6.1A, 6.3B (Santa Maria Della Vittoria, Rome)
Thuringisches Hauptstaatsarchiv Weimar: 3.3A

Every effort has been made to contact copyright holders of material published in this book. Any omissions will be rectified in subsequent printings if notice is given to the publisher.

Thanks also to Michael Mullet of the Department of History, Lancaster University, for his invaluable comments on the original manuscript.

Details of written sources

In some sources the wording or sentence structure has been simplified to ensure that the source is accessible.

E. Cairns, *Christianity Through the Centuries*, Zondervan, 1981: 1.1B, 7.4C
E. Cameron, *The European Reformation*, OUP, 1991: 6.3A, 6.5B
M. Carter, C. Culpin, N. Kinloch, *Past into Present*, Collins, 1989: 7.1D
O. Chadwick, *The Reformation*, Penguin, 1972: 2.1A, 2.5B, 3.2A, 3.3C, 4.3D, 5.1D, 5.2B, 5.2D, 5.3B, 5.3D, 7.2A, 7.2E
N. Cohn, *The Pursuit of the Millenium*, Paladin, 1970: 4.1A, 4.2A, 4.2B
Collins Shorter Contemporary Dictionary, Collins, 1972: 2.2D
J. Davis, *Pursuit of Power*, Harper, 1970: 7.4D
J. Elliott, *Europe Divided*, Fontana, 1968: 7.3E
G. Elton, *Reformation Europe*, Collins, 1963: 3.4A, 5.2C
H. A. L. Fisher, *A History of Europe*, Collins, 1935: 1.1D, 3.3B, 7.1B, 7.3B
V. Green, *Renaissance and Reformation*, Edward Arnold, 1964: 2.1B, 7.1C
W. Hubatsch, *Government in Reformation Europe*, 1971: 3.5B
V. Kiernan, *Crisis in Europe*, Routledge, 1965: 5.1B
J. Kittelson, *Luther and the Reformation*, NP, 1989: 5.1C
R. D. Linder, *The History of Christianity*, Lion, 1990: 1.2B, 1.2C, 2.3B, 2.5C, 3.1C, 3.1E, 3.2B, 4.3B, 6.1B, 6.1C, 6.3C, 6.4D, 6.5A
R. Lockyer, *Henry VII*, Longman, 1968: 2.1C
Niccolò Machiavelli, *Mandragola*, 1517 (this edition published by Greenwood Press): 1.1C
W. H. McNeill, *A World History*, OUP, 1979: 2.2A
A. Maczak, *Politics and Society in Reformation Europe*, 1987: 3.4D
National Geographic, October, 1983, 164(4): 1.1A, 3.1B, 3.2E, 3.2F, 3.2H, 6.2B, 6.4A, 6.5C, 7.4A, 7.5B, 7.5C
Oxford Dictionary of Quotations, OUP, 1979: 3.2C
The Penguin English Dictionary, Penguin, 1972: 2.2C
J. M. Roberts, *History of the World*, Hutchinson, 1980: 2.3C, 3.4B
W. Shirer, *The Rise and Fall of the Third Reich*, Pan Books, 1964: 3.5D
C. Strong, *The Early Modern World*, University of London, 1968: 7.3D
W. Woodruff, *The Struggle for World Power*, MacMillan, 1981: 7.4B

CONTENTS

PART ONE   BACKGROUND TO CHANGE
1.1   Europe in 1517   4
1.2   Christendom   6

PART TWO   A CHANGING WORLD
2.1   Rulers against the Pope   8
2.2   The Renaissance   10
2.3   Printing   12
2.4   New Ideas in the Church   14
2.5   Reasons for Change   16

PART THREE   REVOLT!
3.1   Martin Luther   18
3.2   Rebellion   20
3.3   The Reformation Survives   24
3.4   The Reformation Spreads   26
3.5   The Peasants' War   28
3.6   Life in the New German Churches   30

PART FOUR   THE RADICAL REFORMATION
4.1   The Radical Reformation   32
4.2   Münster, 1535   34
4.3   The Peaceful Revolutionaries   36

PART FIVE   CALVIN AND THE REFORMATION
5.1   Crisis in Switzerland   38
5.2   John Calvin at Geneva   40
5.3   Life in Geneva   42

PART SIX   THE COUNTER REFORMATION
6.1   The Council of Trent   44
6.2   The Inquisition   46
6.3   Mystics in Spain   48
6.4   The Jesuits   50
6.5   Building for God   52

PART SEVEN   CASE STUDIES
7.1   Reformation in the Netherlands   54
7.2   Reformation in France   56
7.3   The Massacre of St Bartholomew's Day   58
7.4   Europe Divided   60
7.5   The Impact of the Reformation   62
Index   64

1.1 Europe in 1517

In the early 16th century, the countries of Europe were not organized in the same way as they are today. For example Germany, which today is one country, was divided up into many little states. Some were ruled by princes, some by dukes, and others were ruled by men who were also bishops and archbishops in the Christian Church. The states were part of what was called the **Holy Roman Empire**. This was not really Roman. It was called this because it was supposed to be the successor of the ancient Roman Empire. The ruler of the Holy Roman Empire in 1517 was **Emperor Charles**, who was King of Spain and who also ruled land in Italy and in what is now the Netherlands and Belgium.

Italy was divided into a number of states. The **Pope**, who was the head of the Roman Catholic Church, ruled land in Italy, just like a prince or a king. These lands were called the **Papal States**. The King of France and Emperor Charles each wanted to rule parts of Italy. There were many wars between them.

In Britain, England and Scotland were separate countries with their own kings. In the east of Europe, **Poland** was much larger than it is today and the Grand Duke of Moscow had succeeded in making his city the centre of a **Russian Empire** which was growing more and more powerful.

People from Europe were beginning to discover more about the world in which they lived. In 1488 the Portuguese explorer, **Bartholomew Diaz**, sailed round the Cape of Good Hope into the Indian Ocean. In 1492 the explorer **Christopher Columbus** sailed from Spain to America. Another Portuguese, **Vasco da Gama**, sailed to India in 1498. Ships belonging to **John Cabot** sailed from Bristol to Newfoundland, in North America, in 1497. Other expeditions went from Spain to South America and from Portugal to East Africa. The European view of the world was changing. The world was much bigger and much more complicated than they had ever imagined. As explorers travelled to different countries, they met many people with different ways of life, ideas and beliefs.

In Europe there was great rivalry between the Christian countries and the **Ottoman Empire**. The Ottoman Empire was based in Turkey, but was conquering countries in Eastern Europe. It was an Islamic empire, but the conquered peoples could continue as Christians if they wished.

A **SOURCE**

Luther's Germany was not two Germanies, as today, but hundreds; a crazy quilt of territories under the Holy Roman Emperor. The seven most powerful states elected the Emperor.

M. Severy, 'National Geographic', 1983, writing about Germany in the early 16th century.

B **SOURCE**

The geographical knowledge of medieval people underwent remarkable changes between 1492 and 1600.

From 'Christianity Through the Centuries' by E. Cairns, 1981.

C **SOURCE**

Do you think that the Turks will invade Italy this year?

A woman character to her priest, in the play 'Mandragola', written by the Italian writer Machiavelli in 1517.

D **SOURCE**

But for the French and Spanish armies, Italy would have been conquered by the Turks.

From 'A History of Europe' by H. A. L. Fisher, 1935.

Under the rule of **Sultan Muhammad II**, Ottoman armies captured the Christian city of Constantinople (modern Istanbul, Turkey) from the Christians in 1453. The Ottomans raided southern Italy and were a constant threat to the Christian west. There were often wars between the Holy Roman Empire and the Ottomans.

Despite this, not all Christian countries opposed the Ottomans. Sometimes the rulers of Venice and France preferred to be friends with the Ottomans and fight the other Christian kings in Europe. We should not think that all Christian rulers were on one side and all Islamic rulers were on the other. The situation in Europe was much more complicated than this in the early 16th century. Many Christian kings were bitter rivals.

Activities...

1 The King of France and the Holy Roman Emperor both wanted to control parts of Italy. Give one advantage and one disadvantage of this for the people of Italy.

2 Read Source B. What kind of evidence might this historian have used to make him write this opinion?

3 a What sort of sources could be used to support the opinion of the historian in Source D?
   b How could you tell that Source A was written before 1990 even if you were not told the date it was published?

Boundary of the Holy Roman Empire

Land ruled personally by the Emperor

0   100   200   300 miles
0   200   400 km

The main countries of Europe and the Holy Roman Empire ruled by the Emperor Charles from 1519.

1.2 Christendom

A

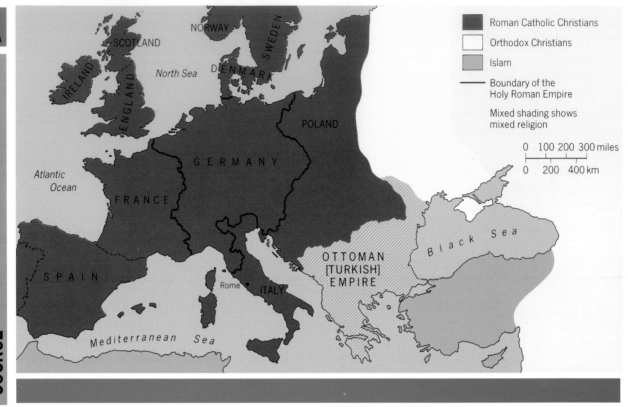

Roman Catholic Christians
Orthodox Christians
Islam
Boundary of the Holy Roman Empire
Mixed shading shows mixed religion

0 100 200 300 miles
0   200   400 km

The religions of Europe in 1500.

SOURCE

At the beginning of the 16th century, the majority of people in Europe were Christians. Those who lived in west and central Europe belonged to the **Roman Catholic Church**. The head of this Church was the **Pope** who lived in Rome. At times there were splits in the Roman Catholic Church – there were two rival popes in 1400 and three in 1409. By the 16th century, however, these splits seemed to have stopped. In what is now Greece and Russia, Christians were members of the **Orthodox Church**. Those who lived in Greece and south-east Europe were ruled by the Turks. The Christian countries were often said to be part of **Christendom**.

The Pope was a powerful ruler as well as a Church leader. He was often involved in politics. Pope Julius II led his army into battle at the siege of the city of Mirandola, north Italy, in 1511 The English Archbishop of York also commanded an army in this war. In 1527 the Christian king Charles V of Spain actually held the Pope as his prisoner. Most popes were Italian. In the 15th century, there were only two popes who were not. Between 1523 and 1978, all the popes were Italian.

B

The nearer you get to Rome the more corruption you will find.

SOURCE

The Italian writer, Machiavelli (1469–1527).

C

Missionary activities in the Middle and Far East, among the Mongols and the Chinese, declined and died out after the middle of the 14th century.

SOURCE

From 'The History of Christianity' by R. D. Linder, 1990.

Most people sincerely believed in God, even if they disapproved of some of the things done by leaders of the Church. During the 15th century, many people paid priests to pray for them after they died. These priests were called **chantry priests**. Pictures and statues of Jesus on the cross became very popular in churches. People were showing that they wanted to feel closer to God; they wanted to be sure that He loved them. When people criticized the Church, it was not because they did not believe any more, it was because they wanted the Church to be better.

A 16th-century painting by the artist Mathis Grünewald, showing the suffering of Jesus on the cross.

D

SOURCE

Activities...

1 According to Savonarola, why were people unhappy with the way that the Church was run? Which other source seems to agree with him?

2 'Source D gives us useful evidence about the beliefs of ordinary people.' Do you agree, or disagree, with this statement? Give reasons for your answer.

3 Look at Sources A and C. Which of these sources would be the most useful for an historian studying the influence of the Christian Church in the late 14th century?

E

SOURCE

The scandal starts in Rome and runs through the whole clergy. They are worse than Turks. They do anything for gold. They only ring their bells for coins and only attend vespers [a church service] when they get something out of it.

Savonarola (1452–98), an Italian monk who was famous for his sermons against the Pope.

2.1 Rulers against the Pope

Although the kings and queens of western Europe were Christians, they sometimes had serious arguments with the Pope. The Church owned land in many countries. The Pope's power was not as great as it had once been, but some rulers disliked the fact that the Pope still seemed rich and powerful. They also felt that they should have the final say in the running of their countries. They resented it when popes tried to interfere. This feeling was often shared by the merchants in the growing towns. Some of them wanted to be free of the control of the Church. Often they had to pay taxes to the Church, which they did not like. Some cities in Germany were actually ruled by bishops of the Church and **clergy** (priests) paid no taxes. This was unpopular.

In a number of countries, powerful kings and queens began to act more freely. This was not new, but during the 15th century it became more common. In England, **King Henry VII** (reigned 1485–1509) was determined to be a strong king. This was continued by his son, **Henry VIII**. In Spain, the same was true of **King Ferdinand** and **Queen Isabella**. The Holy Roman Emperor Charles V was also prepared to go against the Pope if he disagreed with him.

In all these countries the rulers were making the running of the country more organized. They were improving the ways in which taxes were collected and the law courts were run. The people in some of these countries began to feel a real pride in their country. This is called **patriotism**. They began to think of the Pope as a foreigner who interfered in their country. This could be seen in England, Scotland, the Netherlands and in some of the cities of Switzerland and Germany.

The Pope kept more power in countries which were divided, or which were less well run by a weaker monarch. However, even in Scotland where the power of the monarch was weaker, the Church was becoming less powerful.

Since the Pope could not rely on rulers agreeing with him, he had to discuss what he wanted, or **negotiate**, with them. He began to send ambassadors, called **nuncios**, to the courts of the rulers of Europe. The first nuncio was sent to Venice in 1500. Another nuncio was sent to Paris in 1513.

A SOURCE

The Pope was becoming weaker because governments were becoming stronger. And the stronger the government, the more helpless lay the vast wealth of the Church.

From 'The Reformation' by O. Chadwick, 1972.

B SOURCE

Until the election of a pro-Spanish pope in 1591, his relations with successive popes were bad. He was determined to be the absolute master of the Church. Time and again Philip placed the interests of Spain before those of the Roman Catholic Church.

The actions of Philip II, King of Spain. From 'Renaissance and Reformation' by V. Green, 1964.

C SOURCE

Henry was limited by what had been done in the past and by law. Spiritual and moral matters fell within the authority of the Church. These were boundaries which Henry recognized.

The King of England. From 'Henry VII' by R. Lockyer, 1968.

D

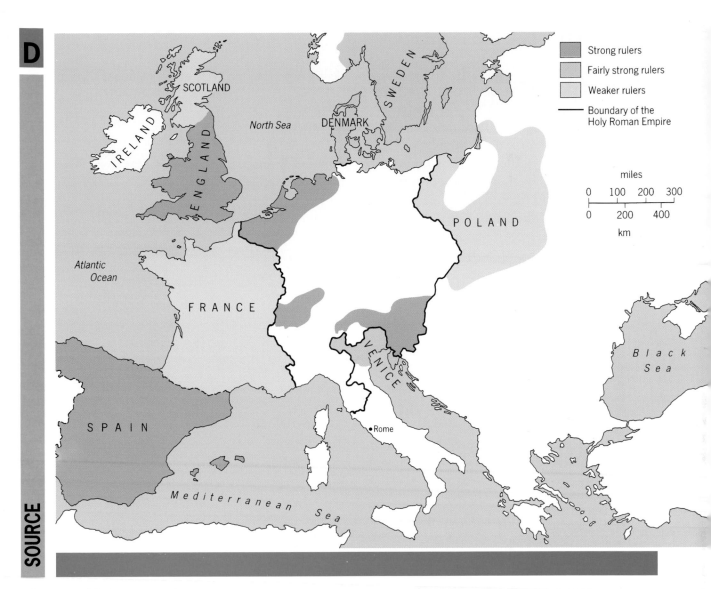

Strong rulers

Fairly strong rulers

Weaker rulers

— Boundary of the Holy Roman Empire

The power of the European rulers in the early 16th century.

E

The King of France has the power to:

• appoint 10 archbishops

• appoint 82 bishops

• appoint 527 abbots.

Rights of the King of France agreed with the Pope by the Concordat of Bologna, in 1516.

Activities...

1 a From all the information in this unit, give three reasons why the power of the Pope was threatened.

  b Why might historians think it important that the Pope started to appoint people as nuncios?

2 Using any of the sources briefly describe:

  a how a king reduced the power of the Pope.

  b how a king respected some of the Pope's power.

  Which of these attitudes towards the Pope was becoming more common in the late 15th/early 16th century?

3 Which of the sources would be the most useful for trying to explain why the power of the Pope was threatened?

2.2 The Renaissance

During the 19th century, historians studied the changes which had taken place in Europe from the 14th to the 16th centuries. They realized that many ideas changed in this particular period of history. One of these changes was that people began to think more about the ideas and ways of life which had been popular with the **Greeks** and **Romans** centuries before. To these 19th-century historians it seemed as if ideas which had been dead for centuries were reborn at this time. As a result, they called this period of history the **Renaissance**. This word means 'rebirth'. Historians still use this word when looking at this period of history, even though they realize that the changes which were happening were very complicated. In fact, many of the old ways of doing things carried on despite the Renaissance.

The interest in ancient Greek and Roman ideas began in Italy. With new enthusiasm, educated people began to search for and study books written centuries before. These people became known as **Humanists**. Some Humanists were important members of the Church. One of these was **Pope Martin V** who became Pope in 1417. Other Humanists were against the way the rulers of the Church tried to control what people studied. They wanted to study and make up their own minds.

In 1480 the Italian **Angelo Poliziano** became Professor of the study of Greek in Florence. This was important because the New Testament was written in Greek by the first Christians. As more people began to study Greek they were able to discover for themselves the message of the Bible. This challenged the authority and power of the Roman Catholic Church. The Church believed that it alone should decide what was right or wrong, even if it differed from what the Bible said. Humanists began to say that people should live in the way written in the Bible, not in the way that the rulers of the Church said.

The ideas of the Renaissance spread to other parts of Europe. A man named **Erasmus** (1469–1536) from Rotterdam (in the modern Netherlands) became a famous scholar. He attacked church leaders who behaved badly and made fun of those people who opposed the new way of studying. In his books ***The Christian Soldier's Manual*** and ***The Colloquies*** he wrote about the way people should behave, in order to please God.

Some of the important cities in Italy during the Renaissance.

A **SOURCE**

The Renaissance had, of course, taken place in Italy from about 1350. With its memories of Roman greatness, it naturally had strong appeal to Italians.

From 'A World History' by W. H. McNeill, 1979.

B **SOURCE**

Erasmus of Rotterdam, painted by
Hans Holbein the Younger, 1523.

C **SOURCE**

The **Renaissance**: the revival
of interest in ancient Greek
art and learning in the 15th
and 16th centuries.

'The Penguin English Dictionary',
1969.

D **SOURCE**

Renaissance: great revival of
learning in the 14th to 16th
centuries.

'Collins Shorter Contemporary
Dictionary', 1972.

Activities...

1 Look at the map and Source A.
  a According to the writer of Source A why did the Renaissance begin in Italy?
  b How could what happened during the Renaissance be used to show that in history ideas do not necessarily get better over time?

2 a In what ways could Sources C and D give you different views about what the Renaissance was?
  b Do you agree with Source C, Source D or neither of these sources? Explain your answer.

3 a What kind of impression do you get of Erasmus from Source B?
  b How might this affect the way in which historians use pictures like this as evidence?

4 a Imagine that you are an important person in the Roman Catholic Church in the late 15th century. Explain why you might be worried about what some of the Humanists are saying and doing.
  b Now imagine that you are a Humanist, like Erasmus. How would you defend what you are doing?

2.3 Printing

 Today we take books for granted. They are produced on machines in their millions. However, before the middle of the 15th century, books were written by hand. This slowed down the spread of ideas. Handwritten books were expensive and few people ever owned one. For most people it was not worth learning to read.

The first people to experiment with printing lived in Asia. In the 5th century, the **Chinese** began to print words and pictures using wooden blocks. The first known printed book was Chinese and it dates from about 868.

Although printing was a very important invention, it does not seem to have spread to Europe. When Europeans experimented with printing in the 15th century they thought that they were doing it for the very first time.

A printing shop, around 1500.

A

SOURCE

In 1445 **Johann Gutenberg** began to print words using **movable metal type**. Letters were cut in metal and fitted together to make words. They were then inked and pressed down on to paper. The very first printed book in Europe was the 'Gutenberg' Bible (1456).

The invention of printing was helped by a number of other inventions. From the 12th century, Italian cloth workers began to experiment with printing patterns on cloth. From the mid-14th century, better quality paper was being made from mashed-up rags. This paper was made for writing but it was eventually used for printing. Neither of these two ways of doing things were deliberately done to make printing happen. But, they smoothed the way for the spread of printing. After Gutenberg began printing in Mainz, Germany, the skill of printing began to spread. There were printing presses in Rome in 1467, Paris in 1470, Cracow (Poland) in 1474, London in 1476.

The new invention led to a huge number of books being produced. These early editions of books are called **incunabula**. By 1550 there were between 15 and 20 million copies of individual books in Europe. The ideas in these books were being spread in a way that had never been known before. When a printer in Paris heard that one of Erasmus' books was about to be banned by the University of the Sorbonne, he quickly printed 24,000 copies. Books were no longer rare. Many people wanted to read them. They wanted to read the ideas for themselves.

SOURCE B

I wish that the Scriptures might be translated into all languages so that not only the Scots and the Irish but also the Turks might read and understand them. I long that the farm labourer might sing them as he follows the plough.

From the writings of Erasmus (1469–1536).

C

The culture which resulted from the coming of printing was as different from any earlier one as it is from one which takes radio and television for granted. The modern age is the age of print.

From 'History of the World' by J. M. Roberts, 1980.

Activities...

1 Match the following **heads** with their **tails**. Each head is a **cause**. Each tail is a **consequence**.

Heads
Printing was invented in Asia.
Gutenberg used movable type.
Books were no longer rare.

Tails
Printing spread over Europe.
More people wanted to read.
The first book was in Chinese.

2 Historians study the thoughts and actions of people in the past. How might the invention of printing affect the view historians have of the past?

3 a Read Source B. How did the invention of printing help Erasmus see his dream begin to come true?
  b Read Source C. Do you agree with this historian's view: 'The modern age is the age of print'? Do you think this has changed since 1980? Explain your answers.

4 What can you learn about the process of printing from Source A?

2.4 New Ideas in the Church

In the 16th century, many people came together to criticize the way that the Church was run. This was not new. For many years, men and women within the Roman Catholic Church had found things about it that they did not agree with.

Some of the people who suggested reforms wanted the Church to be totally changed. They sometimes claimed that leaders of the Church were not true Christians because they were not living the way God wanted them to. This claim was very unpopular with the powerful people in the Church. The leaders of the Church would often accuse their critics of being **heretics**. This meant that they were not real Christians and could be punished for what they said and believed.

In Europe in the 14th century there had been a great disagreement between monks belonging to the Order of St Francis. Some of these monks said that it was wrong for the Church to be so rich and powerful. They claimed that real Christians should live simple lives and not aim to own large amounts of property. These monks were called **Spiritual Franciscans**. In England in the late 14th and 15th centuries there was a group of people known as the **Lollards**. They were followers of **John Wyclif**, who died in 1384. The Lollards read Wyclif's English **translation** of the Latin Bible and used it to condemn the rich and powerful Roman Catholic Church.

In Germany, **John of Wessel** (1400–81) claimed that it was the Bible which should tell people what was right and wrong, not the leaders of the Church. He was arrested and sentenced to life imprisonment in a monastery at Mainz.

A

SOURCE

'Knight, Death, and the Devil' by Albrecht Dürer (1471–1528). It shows that a Christian is like an armed knight fighting all that is bad in the world.

B

It is Jesus who you must love and keep to be your friend. When all else fades away he will not leave you. Whether you want to or not, one day you must leave everything behind. So keep close to Jesus in life as well as in death for only he can help you when everything else fails.

SOURCE

From 'The Imitation of Christ' by Thomas à Kempis (1380–1471).

Some changes in the way that people of the 15th century showed their love for God.

People came to think more about the suffering of Jesus.

More people used rosary beads to help them count and remember their prayers.

People prayed more often to the Virgin Mary.

At Easter, people had processions around their churches. It reminded them of how Jesus carried his cross and was crucified.

Not all Roman Catholics were so revolutionary. Some wanted to change the Church more gradually. These people included members of a movement called the **devotio moderna** (the modern way of serving God). For them it was important to live a holy life, to help the poor and sick and to improve education. One of the early members of this movement was **Geert Groote**, who died in 1384. He formed a community of people who lived in Deventer in the Netherlands. They called themselves the **Brethren of the Common Life**. During the 15th century, they set up communities in Germany and Switzerland.

Thomas à Kempis (1380–1471) was educated by these people. He wrote a very popular book, *The Imitation of Christ*, which encouraged people to have faith in Jesus and to live a life of love as Jesus had done. Many Roman Catholics wanted to try to live 'Christ-like' lives.

Activities...

1 **a** Describe four **different** ways in which people tried to change the Church.
  b Which of these ways would have been least popular with the powerful people in the Church? Explain why.

2 What are the advantages and disadvantages of using a book, like the one quoted in Source B, to find out about the beliefs of members of the Roman Catholic Church in the 15th century?

3 How useful would Source A be to an historian studying Dürer's ideas about what it was like to be a Christian?

4 Use each of the following words in a sentence to show that you have understood their meaning: **heretics**; **Lollards**; **translated**.

5 Look at the cartoons. Which do you think was the most important change?

2.5 Reasons for Change

From 1517 there were tremendous changes in the Roman Catholic Church in Europe. Since almost everyone was a member of the Church, this had a great impact on the lives of ordinary people. Also, because the Church was so powerful politically, the reforms changed the way in which many countries were run. Historians call these great changes the **Reformation**. The changes were so important that the Reformation is sometimes called a **turning point** in the history of Europe. This means that the way in which many people thought and acted changed because of it.

When looking at such an important series of events, historians often ask questions like 'why did this happen when it did?'. They are looking for the **causes** of something happening. Historians divide the reasons why something happened into **long-term** causes and **short-term** causes. Long-term causes are those which have been building up for a long time. Short-term causes are things which happen shortly before an event. Often, people are more aware of the short-term causes because they happen just before a big event or action. However, the long-term causes are just as important.

For a long time, many people had been unhappy with the way in which the Church was run. Some felt that the Pope was too rich and powerful. They felt that he did not rule the Church like a man of God but just like any other rich prince. **Rodrigo Borgia** had even bribed people into making him Pope. As Pope Alexander VI (1492–1503), he did what he could to make his own family rich. This was doubly shocking – priests were not allowed to marry or have sexual partners.

Some priests and monks did not live holy lives. We have seen how men and women began to criticize the Church. Educated people wanted to make up their own minds about the Bible. The ideas of the Renaissance, spread by printing, made them question the right of the Church to tell them how to live their lives.

Since the 13th century, merchants and shopkeepers in towns had become more important. They wanted to make a profit from trade. They resented the way in which the Church controlled people's lives. Some of their views were shared by kings and queens who wanted to reduce the power and wealth of the Church in their countries.

Now that we have got to be Pope, let us enjoy it.

Pope Leo X, when he became Pope in 1513.

A priest known to be guilty of murder was seen to escape with a light imprisonment. A parish priest kept a woman and was not punished. Too many scandals, too many injustices, too much inefficiency.

From 'The Reformation' by O. Chadwick, 1972.

Now no one disagrees with anything that happens. No one opposes anything.

A speaker at the 5th Lateran Council (1517), talking about how nearly everyone at the council agreed that things were all right in the Church.

In the early years of the 16th century, the situation became more tense. Between 1512 and 1517 there were several great meetings of the important people of the Church. This was called the **5th Lateran Council**. It did very little to improve the way the Church was run, however. Pope Leo X, who became Pope in 1513, showed no interest in living a holy life.

The Pope tried to increase the money that German Christians paid to the Church. This was very unpopular in parts of Germany such as **Saxony** where the **cost of living** was already becoming expensive. Despite the fact that many Germans resented giving large amounts of money to the Church it was difficult for them to make a stand against the Pope. Germany was not a united country.

Rodrigo Borgia as Pope Alexander VI (1492–1503). A painting by Pinturicchio.

Activities...

1 Write two headings:
   • long-term causes of unrest
   • short-term causes of unrest.

   Now look at the following list of causes of why the Church was ready for change in the early 16th century. Put each one under one of the two headings. When you have finished, explain how you made your decisions.
   • 5th Lateran Council
   • priests behaved badly
   • rulers wanted more power
   • Pope Alexander VI (Rodrigo Borgia)
   • Pope Leo X
   • cost of living
   • towns wanted more freedom
   • the Church told people what to believe
   • printing was invented
   • the Renaissance.

2 How could Sources B and C be used to give you different views about the state of the Church in the early 16th century?

3 a Read Source B. List two **general** criticisms of the Church that this writer gives. List two **specific** criticisms.
   b Look at Sources B and D. In your opinion which one would be most useful to an historian studying the problems of the Church in the early 16th century? Explain how you decided.

3.1 Martin Luther

In the Middle Ages most Roman Catholics believed that when Christians died they did not go to heaven straight away. Instead their souls went to a place called **purgatory**. In purgatory they were punished for the wrong things that they had done in their lives. When they had been punished enough, they would then go to heaven. People who had lived very bad lives and who were not sorry went to hell. Only the very good went straight to heaven.

Many Roman Catholics believed that it was possible to help a friend or a relative who had died and who was in purgatory. They believed that prayer or a **pilgrimage** to a holy place would help the souls in purgatory. Roman Catholics would also buy **indulgences**. The Church promised that the money they paid would shorten the time that the soul of a dead friend or loved-one had to spend in purgatory.

In 1514 a German nobleman, Albert, became the Archbishop of Mainz, Germany. He paid the Pope a lot of money to get this position. The Pope needed a lot of money in order to build the new church of St Peter in Rome. Albert had borrowed the money he paid the Pope. To get some of it back he arranged to have indulgences sold in his lands. Some of the money he was paid would go to those who had given him loans and some would go to the Pope. The man put in charge of selling these indulgences was a Dominican monk named **Johann Tetzel**.

Martin Luther was a monk at the **University of Wittenberg**. He was the Professor of Biblical Studies. He thought that it was wrong to sell indulgences. He knew that there was no mention of it in the Bible. He also believed that people went to heaven by having faith in God. It was not possible to **buy** forgiveness of wrong doings.

On October 31, 1517 he nailed an essay to the door of the Castle church. In it he gave 95 reasons why he disagreed with Church practice. They are known as the **95 Theses**. His complaints were not revolutionary. They were quite moderate. However, many people were glad to see them. For a long time people in Germany had grown tired of the way the Church was run. The 95 Theses were copied without Luther's permission and they spread across Germany in a few weeks.

A SOURCE

A painting of Luther in the pulpit by Cranach the Elder (1472–1553), one of Luther's friends.

B SOURCE

Martin is a brilliant man. The whole row is due to the jealousy of the monks. It is only a monks' quarrel.

Pope Leo X, in 1518, talking about Martin Luther.

C SOURCE

Today most Roman Catholics and Protestants would say that several generations before Luther's protest against indulgences, there was something radically wrong with the Roman Catholic Church.

From 'The History of Christianity' by R. Linder, 1990.

A 16th-century cartoon about the Roman Catholic Church.

E

SOURCE

One piece of Jesus' baby clothes, one piece of the burning bush, one piece of bread from the Last Supper, five drops of milk from the Virgin Mary.

A list of the so-called 'Holy Relics' that could be seen in the Castle church, Wittenberg, in 1509. It was believed that a visit to this church could save a pilgrim from 1,902,202 years in purgatory.

Luther sent a copy of his protest to Archbishop Albert. Albert was very angry. He decided to 'crush the rash monk of Wittenberg'. He complained to the Pope that Luther was challenging the power of the rulers of the Church. Luther heard how angry the archbishop was, but he refused to **recant**. This means that he would not take back what he had said.

Albert was not the only one against Luther. Johann Tetzel, who sold the indulgences, belonged to a group of monks called **Dominicans**. Luther belonged to a group called the **Augustinians**. There was bad feeling between the two groups of monks and the Dominicans' leader, **Cardinal Cajetan**, joined the attack on Luther.

In 1519 Luther was asked to go to Leipzig to explain himself. Here he met great opposition in an important debate. Faced with these attacks he criticized other things he believed were wrong with the Church. His enemies were pushing him into a corner. He responded by making more criticisms. In 1520 he published a book, ***The Babylonian Captivity of the Church***. In it he accused the Pope of betraying the Christian faith.

Activities...

1 a How many **causes** were there for the argument between Martin Luther and the Church? What are they?
   b Which do you think was the most important?

2 a Did the artist of Source D support Luther or the Roman Catholic Church? Give reasons for your answer.
   b Look at Sources D and E. Which one would be the most useful to an historian studying why Luther acted the way he did? Explain your answer.

3 Read Source B. Was the Pope right? Explain your answer.

3.2 Rebellion

At first Martin Luther had only moderate criticisms of the Church. By 1520 the opposition he faced had turned him into a revolutionary. The Pope sent him a message saying that Luther was in the wrong and demanding that he recant. This type of document is known as a **bull**. Luther took the bull and burnt it by the Old Elster Gate at Wittenberg.

On January 3, 1521 the Pope **excommunicated** Luther. This meant that Luther was thrown out of the Church and that the Pope and other Roman Catholics thought he would go to hell when he died. Nobody should have anything to do with him. In Rome a model of Luther was burned at the stake. This was what his enemies wanted to do to him.

Luther lived in the part of Germany known as **Saxony**. Saxony was ruled by the Elector Frederick. However, Saxony was also part of the Holy Roman Empire. The ruler of the Empire and the lord of Elector Frederick was the Emperor Charles V.

Frederick was an important man. Both the Emperor and the Pope were keen to keep him as a friend. Neither of them wanted to upset him. This helped Luther because Frederick was determined to protect him as one of his subjects. Frederick would not hand Luther over to his enemies. Neither the Pope nor the Emperor could arrest him themselves because this would have annoyed Frederick.

In April, 1521 Luther was ordered to go to a meeting of the leaders of the Holy Roman Empire. The meeting was known as a **Diet**. The Diet that Luther was called to was in the city of **Worms**, Germany. It is known as the **Diet of Worms**. At the Diet, Luther still refused to take back what he had said and written. After he had left the Diet, the members issued an order that Luther was to be arrested and his books burned. No one had arrested him at the Diet because he had **safe conduct** to go there.

A To go against the conscience is neither safe nor right. God help me. Amen.

Luther speaking at the Diet of Worms, 1521, quoted in 'The Reformation' by O. Chadwick, 1972.

B To go against the conscience is neither safe nor open to us. On this I take my stand. I can do no other. God help me. Amen.

Luther speaking at the Diet of Worms, 1521, quoted in 'The History of Christianity', 1990.

C Here I stand. I can do no other. God help me. Amen.

Luther speaking at the Diet of Worms, 1521, quoted in 'Oxford Dictionary of Quotations', 1979.

A painting by Anton von Werner (1843–1915) of the 'The Diet of Worms', 1521.

I am descended from a long line of Christian emperors. A single monk who goes against all Christianity for a thousand years must be wrong.

Emperor Charles V commenting on Martin Luther at the Diet of Worms, 1521.

On the way home from the Diet, Luther was seized by Frederick's soldiers. To protect him from his enemies he was taken to **Wartburg Castle**. No one in Wittenberg knew that he was there. He was given the name 'squire George' to keep his real identity a secret. While he was in hiding he translated the New Testament from Greek into German.

Activities...

1 a Why did the Emperor not arrest Luther?
  b Read Source F and the other information in this unit. What message was Luther giving the Pope when he burned the bull?

2 a Look carefully at Source D. From the way in which this scene is painted, do you think that the artist was for or against Luther? Explain how you reached your opinion.
  b Is Source D a useful source of evidence for what happened at the Diet of Worms in 1521?

3 a Sources A, B and C each claim to report what Luther said. In what ways are they different?
  b Does this mean that these sources cannot be trusted?

Farewell unhappy, hopeless blasphemous Rome! The wrath of God has come upon you as you deserved.

Luther speaking as he burned the bull, 1520.

Martin Luther probably never met the Elector Frederick. Frederick thought that Luther was too revolutionary, but still protected him. Without this protection Luther would probably have been arrested and burned.

While Luther was in Wartburg Castle his friend **Philip Melanchthon** continued to spread Luther's ideas. Both he and Luther wanted the Church to change gradually. They had never intended to break away from the Roman Catholic Church. They still hoped that the Pope would agree with their opinions in time. Melanchthon believed in this even more than Luther.

Other people wanted the Church to change much faster. They were not patient. One of these was **Andreas Karlstadt**. He encouraged the people in Wittenberg to smash the statues in the churches. He accused the people of being **superstitious**. **Nicholas Storch** and **Markus Stübner** also wanted radical change. They were called the **Zwickau Prophets**.

G

In this 16th-century cartoon the devil is shown to be in control of Luther. The man with the musical instrument instead of a nose is meant to be Luther.

Martin Luther heard about what was going on. He could do little to stop it as long as he was in Wartburg Castle. He was very worried by the news. He was afraid that what he had started was getting out of control. There had always been people who wanted to smash the Roman Catholic Church. Luther was not one of these revolutionaries. He wanted to gradually change the Church to make it better. When he heard what was going on in Wittenberg he thought that the changes were going too far and too fast.

Luther was not the only one worried by the situation. Many wealthy and powerful people who supported him were also concerned. They knew that some of the revolutionaries wanted to change more than the Church. For them, changing the Church was just the beginning. They also wanted to change the way in which the country was run. Some wanted to take power and wealth away from the rich. This was not a popular idea with the wealthy people in Saxony.

In 1522 Luther left Wartburg Castle and returned to Wittenberg. He was determined to take control again and stop those who had acted while he was away. Luther wanted to change the things that he thought were very wrong in the Church. He did not want to change everything. Nor did he want the changes to cause violence and upheaval.

Between 1524 and 1525 his worst fears seemed to be proved right. Many thousands of **peasants** rose in revolt against the wealthy landowners. Luther was afraid that his ideas would get linked to this rebellion. He did all he could to show that he did not support the peasants. He encouraged the German rulers to crush the revolt.

Many other people were now having second thoughts about the ideas of the radical reformers. They were afraid that the Church and Germany were breaking apart. By 1525 the writer Erasmus no longer supported Luther. Luther also argued with another reformer named **Zwingli**. They could not agree about **Holy Communion**.

In 1529 the Emperor met with the rulers of the Empire at the **Diet of Speyer**. He threatened to use force against the people in Germany who supported Luther. Some German princes thought this was wrong. They protested to the Emperor. After this the supporters of Luther were called **Protestants**.

Arise, O Lord! Judge your cause. A wild boar is destroying your vineyard.

Pope Leo X in 1520, describing Luther as a 'wild boar' and the Church as a 'vineyard'.

Activities...

4 a Why was Martin Luther so worried when he heard news about what was happening in Wittenberg?
b Why did some people want faster and greater changes than Luther?

5 Why would it be difficult to give a fair description of what Luther did in the 1520s if you only had Sources G and H as evidence?

6 What problems do historians face when they use **cartoons**, like Source G, as evidence in their study of the past?

3.3 The Reformation Survives

In 1530 the leaders of the Holy Roman Empire met once more. This time it was at the **Diet of Augsburg**. Luther could not attend because he had been condemned as an outlaw.

At this meeting it became clear that Emperor Charles V wanted to stop the spread of Protestant ideas. However, he also had other things on his mind. In 1529 Turkish armies had advanced as far as Vienna. The Empire was under threat. The Emperor would have to fight the Turks before facing the problem with the Protestants. The French were also keen to stir up trouble for the Emperor. They encouraged the German Protestants.

In 1531 the Protestant German princes joined together to defend each other. This **alliance** was known as the **Schmalkald League**. The states which joined included **Brandenburg, Prussia, Saxony, Hesse, Mansfeld, Brunswick, Anhalt** and twenty cities. Germany was being split by the ideas of Luther and by the wish of some of the rulers to have more freedom.

B

SOURCE

The Emperor could do little. Affairs in Spain, in Africa, in Italy and in the Netherlands were for him more urgent. Only once in that critical period of twenty years (1521–41) did this king show himself among his German subjects. So, without serious interference the Lutheran faith spread through northern Germany.

From 'A History of Europe' by H. A. L. Fisher, 1935.

A copy of the Schmalkald Treaty, renewed in 1536.

A

SOURCE

The Emperor could not stop them. The Turks advanced again in 1532 and the Emperor was also at war with France. He had fallen out with the Pope, too. In 1527 his soldiers had captured Rome and seized the Pope. The Protestants agreed to help him fight his wars if he left them to practise their religion.

Between 1536 and 1538 the Emperor did badly in his war with the French. In 1539 there was a revolt against his rule in the Netherlands. These difficulties in the Empire protected the German Protestants from being attacked.

In 1541 at the **Diet of Regensburg** any last hopes of peace between the Roman Catholics and Protestants ended. But once again the Emperor could not act. Between 1541 and 1547 he was at war with the Turks again. Also between 1542 and 1544 he was at war with France. He had much to concern him.

Martin Luther died in 1546. At last the Emperor was ready to take action against the Protestants. He persuaded the French to keep out of his quarrel with the Germans. He encouraged disagreements between the German states. The Emperor brought in extra soldiers from his lands in Italy and the Netherlands. In 1547 he finally defeated a Protestant army at the battle of **Mühlberg**.

However, the Emperor was not able to put an end to Protestantism. Some Protestant princes had supported him in the wars against France, and he did not want to attack them. Also, a disagreement broke out between the Emperor and his brother **Ferdinand**. Once more the Emperor had a lot to distract him.

The Protestant prince **Maurice of Saxony** made the most of this. He had supported the Emperor while he crushed rival Protestant states in 1547. Now Maurice broke the friendship. He did this to make Saxony strong as well as to protect Luther's ideas.

Maurice of Saxony persuaded the French king **Henry II** to support him. He also counted on the fact that the Emperor was old and tired. He forced the Emperor to agree to the **Treaty of Passau** (about 1552). This gave Protestant states the right to exist. Another treaty, the **Peace of Augsburg** in 1555, ended the civil war in Germany.

SOURCE C

I do not want to struggle for the Gospel [the 'Good News' about faith in Jesus] by violence and by murder.

From a letter sent by Martin Luther to a friend in the early 1530s.

Activities...

1 'Looking back at the 16th century, the Protestants were bound to have survived. It could not have happened any other way.'
Do you agree or disagree with this statement? Give evidence to support your answer.

2 **a** Read Source C. Did Martin Luther succeed in his aim?
 b Imagine that there is a fire in a museum library. You can only save one of the two sources A and B. Which would you save and why?

3 Make a timeline from 1529 to 1555. Mark on it only those events which you think explain why Protestant ideas survived, even though the Emperor did not like them.

3.4 The Reformation Spreads

The ideas of Martin Luther spread to many other countries in Europe. Luther's ideas were not new. In many countries people had been saying similar things for a long time. The success of the Protestants in Germany encouraged these people.

In Germany the followers of Luther became known as **Lutherans**. In other countries though, not everyone agreed with everything Luther said. Even in Germany there were many people who accepted some of his views but not all of them. This is important to remember. Even though the revolt against the power of the Pope spread, it did not mean that Luther was in control of it. He was not.

Protestant ideas had spread to **Switzerland** by 1518. By 1524 there were Protestant groups in the **Netherlands** and **Hungary**. In **Sweden** the Protestants had taken over the Church by 1527. The same thing happened in **Denmark** and in **Norway** in the 1530s. There were active Protestants in **France** by the 1550s and in **Scotland** by 1560. In Scotland they were led by **John Knox**. By 1552 Protestants had won enough followers among the landowners in **Poland** to stop the government from carrying out the orders of the Roman Catholic Church.

In **England**, matters were more complicated. **Henry VIII** (reigned 1509–47) was against the power of the Pope but made no effort to change the basic beliefs of the Church. During the reign of his son, **Edward VI** (reigned 1547–53), Protestants became more powerful. When Edward died his step-sister **Mary** became queen (reigned 1553–58). She was a devout Roman Catholic. Mary had many Protestants tortured and executed during her reign. She was followed by **Queen Elizabeth I** (reigned 1558–1603) who encouraged Protestantism but did not go as far in changing the Church as some Protestants wanted.

People supported the Reformation for different reasons. We call this having different **motives**. In countries like **Sweden** and **Denmark**, the Reformation was quick and without violence. Here the rulers encouraged the changes. In some countries like **France** and the **Netherlands**, there was a lot of bloodshed. Here the rulers opposed the changes. In **Poland** many landowners supported the Reformation. It was easier for them to do so as they had great power. For years some of the **nobles** had disagreed with the king and the Roman Catholic Church.

A SOURCE

At the Diet of Augsburg (1530) the Protestant princes attended Lutheran services. The Emperor demanded that it should cease. 'Sir,' said the old Margrave of Brandenburg-Ansbach, 'rather than that I should leave off the Word of God, I would kneel here on the spot and lose my head.' Badly taken aback Charles could only stammer, in his broken German: 'My dear lords, no heads off.'

From 'Reformation Europe' by G. Elton, 1963.

B SOURCE

In England a unique relationship arose almost by accident. Henry VIII became entangled with the Pope over his wish to dissolve one of his six marriages in order to remarry and get an heir. With the support of his Parliament, Henry proclaimed himself head of the Church in England and opened the way to the development of an English Church separate from Rome.

From 'History of the World' by J. Roberts, 1980.

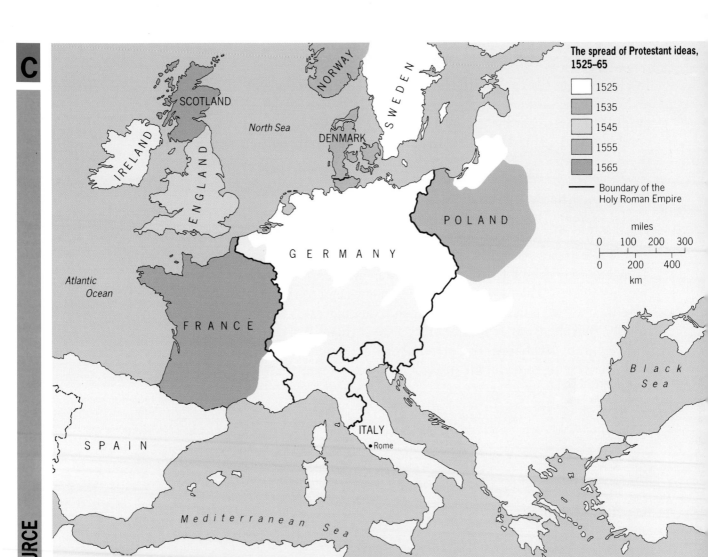

SOURCE

The spread of Protestant ideas, 1525–65

	1525
	1535
	1545
	1555
	1565

— Boundary of the Holy Roman Empire

 D

SOURCE

The power of the local lord was much more real than that of the distant king.

A. Maczak describing the situation in Poland in the mid-16th century. From 'Politics and Society in Reformation Europe', 1987.

Activities...

1 **a** Draw a timeline from 1518–58. Mark on it all of the events given with dates in this unit.

  b Use each of the following words in a separate sentence to show that you have understood their meaning: **Lutherans**; **motives**; **nobles**.

2 Read Sources A, B and D. In what ways do these sources give different impressions about why rulers rebelled against the Pope?

3 Could an historian use Source C as evidence that people all over Europe shared similar beliefs and motives as a result of the Reformation?

3.5 The Peasants' War

 In Germany in the early 16th century, there was a lot of unrest among the **peasants**. Peasants were people who owned small farms. They were hard working. They were becoming more confident and wanted to get rid of anything which stopped them from getting the most out of their farms.

During the **Middle Ages** the peasants had been part of the **feudal system**. This meant that their land was controlled by a local lord. Peasants were often forced to do work for their local lord. They had to pay taxes. They had to use the lord's mill. They had to get the lord's permission if they wanted to move to another village. The peasants wanted to put an end to this system. They were helped by the fact that Germany was so divided that the lords could not unite against them. But this was beginning to change. In different parts of Germany, the lords were trying to bring the peasants under their control once more. This led to trouble.

Peasants looting the Abbey of Weissenau, drawn by Abbot Murer in 1525.

B SOURCE

At the same time, greater burdens than ever were imposed upon the only class of the population which did any really useful work.

From 'Government in Reformation Europe' by W. Hubatsch, 1971.

C SOURCE

The times are so unusual that a prince might get to heaven more easily by killing people than by praying.

Advice from Luther to the lords, in 'Against the Murdering Plundering Hordes of Peasants', 1525.

A SOURCE

In the mid-1470s there was a peasant rebellion in the German state of Würzburg. Here, **Hans Böhm** claimed to have seen visions from God. He claimed that peasants should no longer pay taxes, or give a **tithe** (one-tenth of their crops), to the Church. This idea was very popular with the peasants, but it frightened the lords. Böhm's ideas spread across south and central Germany. Eventually he was arrested and burned.

There were more peasant revolts in the **Rhineland** in 1502, 1513 and 1517. Here the peasants marched under a flag which was decorated with a peasant's clog. They took their name from the German word for this type of shoe: **Bundschuh**. Some of the demonstrations started with simple protests and turned into open revolts which were crushed by the lords.

In 1524 a great peasant revolt swept southern Germany. This happened at the same time as the ideas of the Reformation were beginning to spread. Until 1525 the revolt was not very violent. Most of the peasants only wanted to protect their rights. However, the lords wanted to crush the peasants and caused massacres in many parts of Germany. Approximately 100,000 men and women were slaughtered.

Martin Luther feared that if there were a bloody revolution his Reformation ideas would be lost. In 1525 he wrote a booklet, **Admonition to Peace**. In this booklet he advised the lords to carry out some of the reforms which the peasants wanted. When the peasants' complaints turned into pitched battles, Luther condemned them. In another booklet, **Against the Murdering Plundering Hordes of Peasants**, he advised the lords to smash the peasant revolt.

Some historians feel that Luther encouraged the lords to act with terrible savagery. His last booklet caused him to lose the support of the peasants of southern Germany. They would not forget how he had encouraged the lords to crush them and to destroy their freedom.

At the end of the revolt some of the most violent acts took place in a part of Germany called **Thuringia**. Here **Thomas Müntzer** (1490–1525) encouraged the peasants and workers to attack castles and burn churches. This violence has influenced many later historians' views of the revolt. But in most parts of Germany the peasants acted in an orderly way. It was the lords who turned the revolt into a series of bloody massacres.

D

SOURCE

In what was the only popular revolt in German history, Luther advised the princes to adopt the most ruthless measures against the 'mad dogs', as he called the desperate, downtrodden peasants. Luther employed a brutality of language unequalled until the Nazi time.

From 'The Rise and Fall of the Third Reich' by W. Shirer, 1964.

Activities...

1 a Design a poster which gives the reasons why the peasants wanted to revolt against their lords.

b Now design a poster which might have been produced by a lord explaining why he was crushing the revolt.

2 a What examples of lawlessness can you find in Source A?

b Do you think that the artist agreed or disagreed with what the peasants were doing? Give reasons for your answer.

3 What do you think Source C means?

4 A **consequence** is a result of something happening. Which of the sources in this unit would be most useful for an historian trying to explain the consequences of the revolt for the peasants? Why did you choose this source?

Martin Luther did not intend to start a new Church. He wanted to reform the one he was in. However, as we have seen, the Roman Catholic Church was split by his actions. In some places his ideas were put into practice. In other places they were rejected.

One of the places in which his ideas were eventually accepted was in northern Germany. Here, the churches which refused to accept the authority of the Pope were called **Lutheran**.

The beliefs of the Lutheran Protestants were set down in the **Confession of Augsburg** of 1530. Luther disagreed with many things done by the Roman Catholics, but he only wanted to change what he felt was absolutely necessary. If a way of doing something was not actually banned in the **New Testament**, Luther was willing for it to take place in one of his churches. He was also very keen to work with the German princes. Those who agreed with him he called **'Godly princes'**.

A

SOURCE

Part of a wall painting from a Lutheran church in Germany. It was painted in 1617. This section shows some of the main beliefs of the Lutheran churches.

Martin Luther was a powerful speaker and leader, but he was not a great organizer. However, as it became obvious that the Lutheran churches were going to split from the Roman Catholic Church, he worked hard to replace the old Roman Catholic ideas. In 1526 Luther wrote **Orders of Service** for the German Lutheran churches. These explained how a church service should be run. In 1529 he wrote the **Shorter Catechism**, which explained exactly what Lutherans believed.

Each of the Lutheran churches was run by a group of people called the **consistory**. The first consistory was set up by **John Frederick of Saxony** in 1539. It was responsible for what happened in the Church. The consistory was controlled by the local lord. Some German Christians felt that this situation was not much better than when the Church had been run by the Pope. They argued that the members of the Church should be able to elect their own leaders.

In the new Lutheran churches, **preaching** was a very important part of the church service. The preacher read the Bible and explained what it had to say. For Lutherans, the Bible was the only trustworthy way to find out about God and how they should live their lives. The Lutheran preachers explained that people got to heaven not by being good enough but by believing in God only. This was called **Justification by Faith**. Lutherans rejected any beliefs which were not found in the Bible.

In the Lutheran churches, **hymns** were sung in German instead of in Latin. Ministers of the Church were allowed to marry. In 1525 Luther married Catherine von Bora. She had once been a nun. Roman Catholic priests could not marry. Luther also believed that ordinary people should be given both bread and wine at Communion. In the Roman Catholic Church, ordinary people were just given bread; only the priests were given bread and wine.

Activities...

1 **a** Write a definition for each of the following: **Godly prince**; **consistory**; **Justification by Faith**.
   b Explain how each of these affected the lives of people in the new Lutheran churches.

2 Complete the table below, identifying the beliefs of Lutherans shown in Source A.

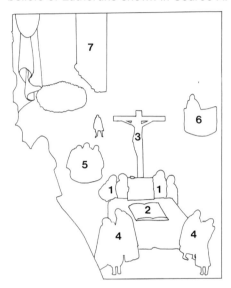

Number	Explanation
1	Pictures of Matthew, Mark, Luke and John, the writers of the four gospels. The gospels tell the story of the life of Jesus in the Bible.
2	
3	
4	
5	
6	
7	

3 What important Lutheran beliefs are not shown in Source A?

4 Why might Germans have wanted to paint and look at a picture like Source A in 1617?

4.1 The Radical Reformation

Luther was not the only person preaching new ideas in the 1520s. Others were also questioning the right of the Pope. Historians sometimes call these people members of the **Radical Reformation**. They were far more revolutionary than Luther.

Some of these people were known as **Anabaptists**. This word describes many different groups of people. Although they were not part of one organization, they often shared some beliefs. For example, they all thought that only adults should be baptized and not children. This was because adults were able to say what they believed in. Many of them thought that it was wrong to use violence, and that no one should be *forced* to believe anything. Most also believed that members of a church should elect their own leaders and that Christians should live pure lives. Some of them went further and said that Christians should share all they owned with each other.

In 1525 Anabaptists led by **Conrad Grebel** met in Zürich. They were threatened by other Protestants in the city. The people against the Anabaptists did not want a revolution in the Church. One of the Anabaptist leaders, **Michael Sattler**, was burnt at the stake. He was killed by other Protestants, not Roman Catholics.

Soon, Anabaptist groups were springing up all over Germany. Some were started when the Swiss Anabaptists fled to Germany. The Anabaptist leader, **Balthasar Hubmaier**, had to escape to Moravia (in modern Czechoslovakia). He persuaded many people to join him. In 1528, he was burnt at the stake in Vienna. His wife was executed by drowning. They were killed by Roman Catholics.

A SOURCE

Anabaptism was never centrally organized. There existed some 40 independent sects, each grouped around a leader who claimed to be an inspired prophet.

From 'The Pursuit of the Millenium' by N. Cohn, 1970.

B SOURCE

1 All those who have left their children unbaptized must have them baptized within eight days.
2 Whoever baptizes an adult will be drowned without mercy.

Laws of the city of Zürich in Switzerland, from 1525 and 1526, against the Anabaptists.

The main Anabaptist beliefs.

Adults only should be baptized.

Anabaptists should not use violence if attacked.

Church members could vote and control how the Church was run.

Many Protestant leaders feared the revolutionary Anabaptists. Luther openly quarrelled with them in 1535. Roman Catholics and Protestants alike attacked them.

Two famous preachers accused of being Anabaptists were **Thomas Müntzer** (1489–1525) and **Niklas Storch**. They were not in favour of peace. They declared that the poor should destroy the rich.

Müntzer and Storch began to preach at Zwickau, Germany. Many of the town's silver miners supported them. There was a lot of unemployment around the town and prices were rising. Poorer people were insecure and frightened by this.

In 1521 they were **expelled** from Zwickau by the town authorities. They travelled and preached that the powerful rulers should be swept away. Many peasants supported them, as did the copper miners in a part of Germany called **Thuringia**. This was at the time of the Peasants' War (see Unit 3.5). Müntzer led a peasant uprising in 1525. He was condemned by Luther. An army led by the German princes crushed his revolution, killing 5,000 peasants and miners in a bloody massacre. Müntzer was beheaded.

Despite these setbacks, the Anabaptists remained popular among many poorer people. They were impressed by the faith and determination of the Anabaptists. They wanted to have a say in how their Church and country was run. The peasants felt betrayed by Luther who had supported the princes during the Peasants' War.

Anabaptist sayings from the mid-16th century.

Activities...

1 **a** Write out the following events in **chronological** order (the order in which they happened):
   - Peasants' War
   - execution of Sattler
   - Müntzer expelled from Zwickau
   - Hubmaier in Moravia
   - first Anabaptists in Zürich.

   b Write down the following headings: 'Why people supported the Anabaptists' and 'Why people opposed the Anabaptists'. Under each heading, list all the reasons you can think of.

2 Source A was written by an historian. Using the information in this unit explain why it is difficult for an historian to describe the beliefs of the Anabaptists.

3 Read Sources B and C. Which source gives you the best evidence for why the Anabaptists were different from other Protestants? Explain your answer.

All beliefs should come from the Bible.

Anabaptists would not use force to make people agree with them.

4.2 Münster, 1535

For almost 200 years after the 1520s the word 'Anabaptist' was used to describe any dangerous person who threatened to break up society. This was partly because Anabaptists refused to obey the government when it told them what they should believe. Government leaders were frightened that if people were free to choose their own religion they might soon want to choose their own government. Also some Anabaptists were very revolutionary. They led attacks on the way society was ruled. Perhaps the wildest and most famous attack took place in Münster, a city in north-western Germany.

Münster was ruled by a Roman Catholic bishop. Many people in the city were not happy about this. The priests did not pay taxes like other citizens. The bishop stopped the merchants from running the town in the way they wanted to. During the Peasants' War, the citizens forced the bishop to give them more power. When the war was over he broke these promises.

By 1532 there was also plague in the area. The harvests had been poor and taxes were increasing. People were unhappy. In 1532 supporters of Luther took control of the town. Many rich merchants supported them. The bishop was unable to stop the take-over.

The situation soon got out of control. Many poor people flooded into Münster. Most came from the Netherlands. Many were unemployed cloth workers. They were desperate and wanted change. One of these newcomers was **Jan of Leyden**, who was an Anabaptist and a revolutionary.

Jan of Leyden soon won the right for people in Münster to believe in what they wanted. This is called **liberty of conscience**. This attracted many other extreme Anabaptists to the city. The richer citizens were afraid and left the city. Churches were robbed. Jan proclaimed that God would soon destroy all the world, saving only Münster. Jan was joined by another Anabaptist leader, **Jan Matthys**.

In February 1534, the bishop tried to recapture the city. He surrounded it with soldiers. The **siege** lasted until June 1535. In the city anyone who disagreed with the Anabaptist leaders was killed. Money was banned. All food had to be shared. All books were destroyed, except the Bible.

A **SOURCE**

There is evidence to suggest that the unemployed were both more numerous and more desperate than in earlier centuries.

A description of the cloth workers in the Netherlands from 'The Pursuit of the Millenium' by N. Cohn, 1970.

B **SOURCE**

And so they came, the Dutch and the Frisians and scoundrels from all parts who had never settled anywhere. They flocked to Münster.

An eyewitness account of events in Münster, 1533.

C **SOURCE**

Slay all monks and priests, and all sovereigns in the world; since our king alone is the true sovereign.

War song of the Münster Anabaptists, 1535. The king was Jan of Leyden.

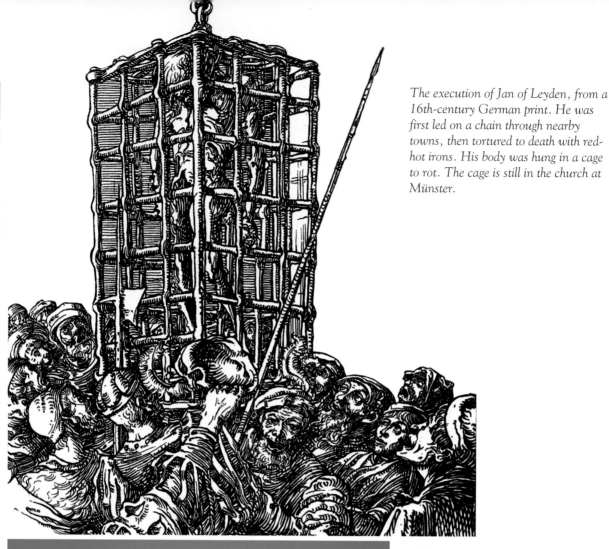

The execution of Jan of Leyden, from a 16th-century German print. He was first led on a chain through nearby towns, then tortured to death with red-hot irons. His body was hung in a cage to rot. The cage is still in the church at Münster.

At Easter 1534, Jan Matthys was killed in a battle. He had gone to battle with only a few people because he thought that God had told him to do this. Jan of Leyden announced that he was **King of the New Jerusalem**. He lived in luxury. Jan had fifteen wives. He killed anyone who disagreed with him, and women who argued with their husbands were executed. Jan promised the citizens that the cobblestones would turn to bread. They did not and the people starved.

At last the bishop's soldiers succeeded in getting into the city. Jan of Leyden was captured and executed in January 1536. The bishop had him tortured with red-hot irons. Jan died without making a sound.

The Anabaptists at Münster were different from most Anabaptists. Most Anabaptists would not use violence. They would not force people to do something. But for years, the events in Münster affected how people thought about Anabaptists.

Activities...

1 a Make a list of the different reasons why there was a revolt in Münster.

   b Look carefully at your list. Arrange your reasons in order of importance: the most important at number one. Explain how you made your decisions.

2 Read Source A. Can you find any evidence in this unit to support this historian's opinion?

3 Why might the Bishop of Münster have chosen to punish Jan of Leyden in the way described in Source D?

4.3 The Peaceful Revolutionaries

Most Anabaptists were not violent. They wanted to live peaceful lives. After the terrible things that happened at Münster, many rejected all violence.

One of the leaders of these peaceful Anabaptists was **Menno Simmons** (1496–1561). He had been a Roman Catholic priest in the part of the Netherlands known as **Friesland**. In 1536 he left the Roman Catholic Church and became a travelling preacher.

The people who accepted his ideas are called **brethren** or **Mennonites**. Mennonites were Christians who refused to use any kind of violence, following the teachings of Jesus. They thought that local groups of Christians should run their own affairs. They also thought that Christians should not get involved in politics. In their services they washed one another's feet. This reminded them that like Jesus they had to love and care for each other. They greeted each other with a **kiss of peace**.

Menno Simmons (1496–1561).

A Hutterite family, 1589.

A

SOURCE

If anyone disobeyed these ideas they were punished by being **shunned**. This meant that no other Mennonite would have anything to do with them. In Germany and the Netherlands, there was a split in the Mennonite movement. This was about how strict punishments should be for anyone who broke the rules. The strictest Mennonites totally ignored those who broke the rules.

Other peaceful Anabaptists were to be found in southern Germany and in modern Czechoslovakia. These were led by **Jorg Cajob**. Many had escaped from **persecution** in the 1520s. At this time, many Anabaptists had been killed because of their beliefs.

These Anabaptists lived together in a **Brüderhof**. In English this means 'brotherhouse'. All the families in a Brüderhof shared what they owned or earned with the other families. These people came to be called **Hutterites** in the 1530s, after one of their leaders, **Jakob Hutter**.

The Hutterites tried to make everything that their little communities needed. This is called being **self-sufficient**. By the early 17th century, they had a reputation as being honest and peaceful craftworkers. They became famous as **doctors**, **clock makers** and **furniture makers**.

In the 1620s a fierce war began in Europe. It was called the **Thirty Years War**. During this war Roman Catholic soldiers destroyed the peaceful Hutterite communities. The survivors fled to the Turkish lands.

C SOURCE

Private property is the greatest enemy of love. The true Christian must get free from owning property, if they want to become a disciple [of Jesus].

Extract from a Hutterite leaflet from 1545.

D SOURCE

We think that it is wrong to buy something and sell it to make a profit. This makes the thing more expensive to poor people. To do this takes the bread from their mouths.

Extract from a Hutterite leaflet from about 1540.

Activities...

1 a What did the Mennonites believe?
  b During the 16th century, the enemies of the Mennonites kept calling them Anabaptists. Why might they have done this?
  c Washing a person's feet and kissing them in a service were unusual things to do. Why might the Mennonites have done these things?

2 In the 16th century, there were no daily newspapers. Imagine that there were and that you were a reporter in 1589. Your editor has asked you to write 100 words about the Hutterites.

Using the information in this unit write your article. You can also include your own opinion of these people.

3 a Read Source B. In your own words describe Menno Simmons' opinion of those people who used violence against others.
  b Read Sources B, C and D. An historian might think there are problems in using just these sources as a way of finding out about the people studied in this unit. Explain some of these problems.

5.1 Crisis in Switzerland

At about the time that Luther was beginning the Reformation in Germany, changes were also happening in **Switzerland**. In this country the person who began the changes was **Huldreich Zwingli** (1484–1531).

Zwingli studied in the Swiss cities of **Basle** and **Berne**. He became **vicar** of the church in the city of **Glarus**. He was also the **chaplain** to one of the Swiss armies. This meant that he took care of the religious needs of the soldiers. These soldiers would fight for whoever paid them. They were called **mercenaries**. As their chaplain, Zwingli was present at two battles.

Zwingli was very **patriotic**. This means that he was very proud of his country. He wanted the Swiss to be free from the rule of other countries.

In Germany, Luther at first did not want to break away from the Roman Catholic Church. In Switzerland, Zwingli wanted a complete break.

Religious divisions in Switzerland at the time of Zwingli's death, 1531.

A

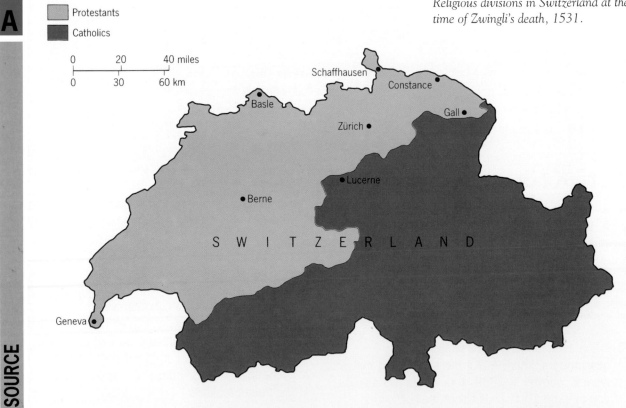

Protestants

Catholics

SOURCE

Zwingli met **Erasmus** in 1515. He was impressed with Erasmus' ideas. In 1518 Zwingli became priest at the **Great Minster**, in **Zürich**, where he began his reforms. Like Luther he worked with the people who ran the city. In 1522 he married **Anna Meyer**.

In 1523 there was a great debate between Zwingli and the Roman Catholic **Bishop of Constance**. Zwingli explained his beliefs. They were that a person only got to heaven through faith in God; the Bible was the only sure way to find out about God; and that ministers of the Church should be able to marry.

The town council of Zürich heard Zwingli defend his ideas. They decided that he was right. They allowed priests and monks to have wives. Anything done in the churches which was not taught in the Bible they banned.

In 1528 Zwingli took part in another debate. This time it was in **Berne**. After he explained his ideas, the Swiss cities of **Basle**, **Gall**, **Schaffhausen** and **Constance** joined him.

In 1529 Zwingli and Luther had a disagreement. At the **Conference of Marburg** they could not agree about what they believed about Holy Communion. They could not overcome their differences. As a result, the German princes would not support Zwingli's Reformation. Instead they supported Luther.

Zwingli was very different from Luther. He did not respect history the way Luther did. Zwingli wanted to change the Church in many ways. In Zürich, organs, pictures and statues were removed from churches. This was because Zwingli thought they were wrong and distracted people from the worship of God. Church services became very simple. Everything that happened in a service had to be mentioned in the Bible.

Not everyone in Switzerland agreed with Zwingli. Some people preferred to stay Roman Catholic. The Roman Catholic areas of the county were called the **Forest Cantons**. The Forest Cantons sent an army to attack Zürich. In 1531 Zwingli died fighting for his ideas at the battle of **Kappel**. As a result of this battle, the different areas of Switzerland were left to choose their own beliefs. The country was divided.

Heinrich Bullinger (1504–75) became the next leader of the Swiss Reformation. In 1549 the Protestants who followed Bullinger united with other Protestants living in Geneva.

SOURCE D

The change of appearance and worship in the Swiss churches was more revolutionary than in the churches of northern Germany.

From 'The Reformation' by O. Chadwick, 1972.

Activities...

1 Read Source D and the other information in this unit. In what ways was Zwingli's Reformation more revolutionary than Luther's?

2 Look at Source A. What are the advantages and disadvantages in using a map like this to find out about people's beliefs?

3 a How might the information in Source B help to explain the kind of man Zwingli was?

b Source C records one of Luther's many comments. Why might an historian think this one was particularly important?

4 Imagine you are organizing the publicity for one of Zwingli's debates. Design a poster setting out his ideas and encouraging people to come along and listen to him.

5.2 John Calvin at Geneva

The death of Zwingli at the battle of Kappel stopped the growth of Reformation ideas in Switzerland and its region. But from 1536, changes began again. This time they were started by a Frenchman, **John Calvin** (1509–64).

Calvin had first come across the ideas of Martin Luther while he was a student in Paris. In 1533, after much thought, he finally left the Roman Catholic Church. He went to the Swiss city of **Basle**. Many other French people lived in this city. Here he wrote a book which explained his ideas about God. It is called ***The Institution of the Christian Religion***. It is usually called, for short, ***The Institutes***.

Calvin's ideas had a tremendous impact on many people. Like Luther and Zwingli he believed that when Christians wanted to know about God, they should turn to the Bible and not the Pope. He also believed that people could only experience God if God chose to show Himself to them.

Calvin believed that men and women were unfit for heaven. He believed that their very nature was **sinful**. At the beginning of time God had decided that some people were going to go to heaven. The rest were going to hell. Who went to heaven was God's decision. It had nothing to do with the actions or ideas of the people. This belief is called **predestination**.

B Good-bye Geneva. In the end the King of France himself will be a citizen here.

A comment by one of the enemies of Calvin, in the 1550s.

C The easy-going unstable city of the past emerged as a grim, solid community of psalm-singing church go-ers. Calvin's Geneva should be treated seriously as an awful warning.

SOURCE

From 'Reformation Europe' by G. Elton, 1963.

D If he once gets his knife into you, you do not stand a chance.

Comment by one of the other Church leaders in Geneva in the 1550s. It describes the way in which Calvin dealt with people who disagreed with him.

A

SOURCE

A sketch of Calvin drawn by one of his students during a lecture. It dates from the 1550s.

In 1536 Calvin was invited to live in **Geneva**. The leader of the Reformation there was **Guillaume Farel**. He asked Calvin to help him. But Calvin was not popular in Geneva and was forced to leave. Many Swiss people disliked being told what to believe by a foreigner. In 1541 he was invited to go back. Even then many people were not happy. It was not until 1555 that he was finally in control of the Church in the city.

Calvin wanted to make Geneva a **city of God**, where everything was run the way Calvin and his supporters thought was right. The city laws were changed to stop sinful behaviour. Calvin tried to make sure that the Church controlled the lives of all the citizens. In Geneva, Calvin's Church often clashed with the government.

Geneva became the home to many people whose beliefs had been banned in their own countries. They came to Geneva because they agreed with Calvin. A school was set up to teach **theology**. This is the study of God and ideas about God. The school was called the **Geneva Academy**. Calvin set out his ideas in a more orderly way than Luther did. Also, unlike Luther, he always thought out carefully what he was going to say, write and do.

John Knox, the leader of the Reformation in Scotland, commenting on the Geneva Academy in the 1560s.

E

SOURCE

A portrait of Calvin.

Activities...

1 a In your own words explain what Calvin believed about human nature.
  b How did this affect the way he tried to run Geneva?
  c The writer of Source B lived in Geneva before Calvin arrived. The writer of Source F went there to escape from persecution in his own country. How might this help to explain their different opinions of Calvin?

2 Does Source C give you **facts** or **opinions** about life in Geneva? Explain how you decided.

3 a How useful is Source D to an historian?
  b How useful are Sources A and E ?

5.3 Life in Geneva

John Calvin's ideas affected the way that people lived in the city of Geneva. He believed that the Church should carefully control the lives of the citizens. This would stop wrong things from being done. Problems arose because not everyone agreed with him about what was wrong.

Calvin's church was well-organized. In 1541 he laid down how it should be run. This was explained in his **Ecclesiastic Ordinances**. Ecclesiastic is another word for 'church'. Ordinances means 'rules'.

The rules stated that there were four different leaders in the Church. Some were called **pastors**. Their job was to preach and control the Church. Some were called **teachers**. Their job was to make sure that people believed the right things. Some were called **deacons**. Their job was to look after the poor. All these jobs were done by men. People who are not full-time ministers are called **lay people**. Some lay people could become **elders**. The elders helped to run the Church. This kind of organization is known as a **Presbyterian Church**. The leaders met together every Thursday in a group called a **consistory**.

Calvin's idea of the Church was not **democratic**. The ordinary people did not run the Church. Pastors were chosen by other pastors and not by the people. The elders of the Church in Geneva tried to make sure people behaved properly. This was not a new practice. The old Roman Catholic bishops had also tried to control the way people lived.

Between 1541 and 1546 in Geneva, 58 people were executed for disagreeing with the Church. A further 76 were thrown out of the city. In 1546 taverns (modern pubs) were made illegal. In 1547 it was made illegal to wear fashionable trousers. A law against dancing was passed in 1550. The pastors were given the right to visit every home in Geneva, to make sure that people were living the way they had been told.

However, Calvin did not have total control. The **City Council** had the power to stop a man becoming a pastor. People could only be executed or expelled if the council agreed. Despite Calvin's complaints, taverns were reopened. An attempt to force people to have only Biblical names was also rejected by the council. The council complained if the pastors preached for too long.

A **SOURCE**

The way things are organized does not mean that the pastors have any power in the Government.
The Church does not have the authority to interfere with magistrates and the courts.

Church rules of Geneva in the 1540s.

B **SOURCE**

They thought of themselves as responsible for the protection of old people, orphans, widows, children, the sick.

From 'The Reformation' by O. Chadwick, 1972.

C **SOURCE**

We are like dogs, who bark when our master is attacked.

A comment made by a member of the Church consistory of Geneva in the 1540s.

Some members of the council were also members of the Church consistory. This suggests that Calvin only succeeded because enough important people in Geneva supported what he was doing.

Calvin was also helped by the many French people who fled to Geneva. They had been punished for their beliefs in France. In Geneva they supported the changes brought about by Calvin.

SOURCE

Someone said that the arrival of the French refugees put up the cost of living. A woman tried to cure her husband by tying round his neck a walnut containing a spider. Another danced. A woman of 62 married a man of 25.

Complaints about some Geneva citizens discussed by the consistory on 16 February, 1542.

Some of the changes Calvin brought to churches in Geneva:

- Anything not mentioned in the Bible was banned from church services.
- Simple churches. No ornaments or statues. No robes for the pastors.
- Members took Holy Communion around a table. There was no altar.
- Congregations sang hymns but they were not accompanied by musical instruments.

Activities...

1 In Geneva in the 1550s there was no Tourist Information service. Imagine that there was one and that you are putting together a simple guide for tourists with advice and illustrations. In your guide describe:
  - how the city is organized
  - what church services are like
  - who Calvin is
  - what kinds of behaviour to avoid.

In your guide you should also attempt to explain to visitors why the city is run the way it is. You may refer to any of the information in this unit. You may also want to look again at the information in Unit 5.2.

2 a Read Source B. Does this historian give you a good or bad impression of the work of the Geneva consistory?

b Which other source gives a similar account of the consistory as being protectors of people?

3 In 1564 Calvin said, 'The people of Geneva have always feared me more than they loved me.' Using any of the sources, give reasons why this might have been so.

4 'John Calvin was a dictator!' Use the information in this unit to decide whether you agree or disagree with this statement. Give reasons for your answer.

6.1 The Council of Trent

When Martin Luther first started to complain about the Roman Catholic Church the Pope did not realize how serious it was going to be. **Pope Leo X** had other things on his mind: he was involved in politics, he was keen on hunting and gambling, and he spent a lot of time and money buying works of art. He hoped to get rid of Luther without much bother. He was wrong.

By 1520 the leaders of the Roman Catholic Church were beginning to realize they had made a mistake. Luther was not going to go away. He had become famous. The Church was splitting apart.

Some Roman Catholics realized there were problems in the Church. In 1517 a society called the **Oratory of Divine Love** was started in Rome. Its leaders were Roman Catholics who thought that some things should change in the Church. One of its members was **Gasparo Contarini**. He was born in 1483 and became a **cardinal** in 1535. A cardinal is a high-ranking person in the Roman Catholic Church.

Luther is a drunken German. He will feel different when he is sober.

A comment made by Pope Leo X in 1518.

The Council of Trent (1563).

Contarini was a peacemaker. He tried to heal the split with the Lutherans. In Italy some Roman Catholics called him a traitor. He failed to bring the two sides together.

People such as Contarini believed that the Roman Catholic Church had to change. If it did not change, other people would follow Luther and leave the Church. If it were to survive, the Roman Catholic Church would have to show that it could improve itself. This attempt to improve the Roman Catholic Church is known as the **Counter Reformation**.

In 1523 Clement VII (Leo X's brother) became Pope. He tried to reform the Church but found it was not easy. He could not get the Roman Catholic King of France and the Roman Catholic Holy Roman Emperor to agree with one another. They were bitter rivals. This situation made it hard to unite the Church.

In 1534 Pope Clement died and was replaced by Pope Paul III. He tried to stop **bribery** in the Church. He tried to make people obey **Church laws**. He tried to make **monks** live holier lives. He tried to ban **prostitutes** from the city of Rome.

Pope Paul was only successful with a few of these reforms. However, he did do something very important. He called together a great meeting of the Roman Catholic Church. It was called the **Council of Trent**.

The Council met in the city of Trent in northern Italy. It had three meetings: 1545–47, 1551–52 and 1562–63. Most of the people who came were from Italy, Spain and the lands of the Holy Roman Empire. Even some Protestants attended. In 1552, when they saw they could not agree with the Roman Catholics, they left.

The Council of Trent made it clear that none of Luther's basic points would be listened to. Indulgences could no longer be sold, but were still seen as good and useful. The Pope was still going to be the head of the Church. The Roman Catholic Church still taught that people could get to heaven by what they did as well as by what they believed. The Protestant ideas (**doctrines**) were rejected. The Pope was stronger than ever. Roman Catholic ideas were being defended and publicized.

SOURCE **C** The Roman Catholic Church seemed to be unaware of the widespread unrest among the faithful, which Luther's protest represented.

From 'History of Christianity' by R. Linder, 1990.

Activities...

1 When Luther first heard about the Council of Trent he said: 'The [Roman Catholic] Church cannot be reformed.'
  a From what you have read in this unit, why do you think he said this?
  b In your opinion was he being fair?

2 a Which of the following statements are **facts** and which are **opinions**?
  • Luther was a good man.
  • Clement was a Pope.
  • Contarini was a cardinal.
  • Roman Catholics ignored Protestants.
  • Trent is in Italy.
  • Contarini was a peacemaker.
  b Read Source C. Do you think that this refers to Pope Leo or to the popes who came after him? Explain how you decided.

3 a Look at Source A. What impression does this picture give you of the Roman Catholic Church?
  b How could an historian use Source B to show that Pope Leo was responsible for the Church being split in the 1520s?

6.2 The Inquisition

Many people who opposed the Roman Catholic Church found themselves facing the **Inquisition**. This was a special type of court. Most courts only examine a person's **actions**. In the Inquisition courts, the judges also tried to judge the thoughts in a person's mind. Their aim was to find and punish people who disagreed with the Roman Catholic Church and its leaders.

The Inquisition was not started just to get rid of Protestants. It had existed for many years. Its official name was the **Supreme Sacred Congregation of the Holy Office**. It used torture to get information and employed secret agents. After 1224, people found guilty by the Inquisition could be executed by the rulers of the country in which the trial had taken place.

Many of the leading members of the Inquisition were from the **Dominican** order of monks. It was the Dominicans who had led the opposition to Martin Luther in Germany. They would have sentenced him to be burned, if they had been able to catch him.

People who disagreed with the Church were accused of being **heretics**. If two witnesses accused someone of being a heretic, that person would be arrested. Often the person was not told the charge or who had made the accusation. Any lawyer who tried to defend the accused person was likely to be arrested as well. Trials often lasted a long time. During this time the accused person was kept in prison.

People found **guilty** of being heretics were punished in different ways. The least serious punishments were to go on a **pilgrimage** or to go to a certain number of **church services**.

B

SOURCE

Even if my own father were a heretic, I would gather wood to burn him.

A comment made by Pope Paul IV in the 1550s.

A

SOURCE

Those found guilty of more serious 'crimes' were **whipped**. Others were **fined** or had their property **confiscated**. If a person refused to give up his or her beliefs, they would be **executed**. Often they were **burnt at the stake**. This was done by the local representatives of the ruler of the country. The Church did not actually do the killing.

During the Reformation many people turned against the Pope. The Inquisition was very active after 1541. In Roman Catholic countries it was used to prevent people from turning against the Roman Catholic Church. The Inquisition was led by a man named **Cardinal Caraffa** who later became Pope Paul IV. The Inquisition was most powerful where most of the population was Roman Catholic. It found it difficult to work in places where many people were Protestants, or if the ruler were sympathetic to Protestants. It did most of its work in **Italy**, **Spain** and **France**. Some rulers used the Inquisition to get rid of people they did not like. In Spain and France the rulers had a lot of control over the actions of the Inquisition. Sometimes, however, it was more complicated. In 1547 King Henry II of France wanted to use the Inquisition. The French parliament would not let him. They thought they would lose their power to the Inquisition.

In 1559 Pope Paul IV issued a list of books which the Roman Catholic Church thought were written by heretics. This was called the *Index*. A longer list of books was published by Pope Pius IV in 1564. This list included three-quarters of all the books printed in Europe at the time. Mostly the *Index* was a failure. People still printed and bought books that had been banned.

Activities...

1 **a** Explain some of the reasons why the Inquisition was successful in some countries but failed in others.
  b In your opinion which was the most important reason for success? Explain your answer.
  c Which was the most important reason for failure? Explain your answer.

2 Not all the men in the procession in Source A were members of the Inquisition. Which ones do you think were? Give reasons for your answer.

3 Source A shows a crowd watching the burning of heretics in Spain. It also shows the members of the Inquisition in grand procession. Does it prove the Inquisition was popular in Spain?

Members of the Inquisition in procession in Spain and the burning of heretics. From a Spanish enquiry, 1560.

6.3 Mystics in Spain

Protestants were not the only people who wanted a closer relationship with God. Many Roman Catholics wanted this too.

In Spain, **Teresa of Ávila** (1515–82) believed that it was possible to have a direct, personal experience of God. This idea was not new. Teresa is sometimes called a **mystic**. Mystics believe that by living holy lives of prayer, people can feel and enjoy the presence of God.

Teresa was a member of the **Carmelite Order** of nuns. In the 1550s she was very ill. During this time she believed she saw God. This is called a **vision**. After this experience she tried to encourage the other nuns to live purer lives. She travelled far and wide in Spain. In 1562 she set up a new community of nuns at the town of **Ávila**. When she died in 1582, she had started seventeen new communities.

A

SOURCE

The difference between the Roman Catholic and Protestant Reformation was between gradual and sudden change.

From 'The European Reformation' by E. Cameron, 1991.

B

SOURCE

'Ecstasy of Saint Teresa' by Bernini (sculpted 1644–52). This statue was made to show Teresa experiencing a vision of God's love.

Some Roman Catholics distrusted Teresa. They felt that if a person had a direct relationship with God, they might not need the priests of the Church. Although Teresa was a Roman Catholic, she worried many powerful Church members. In 1561 the **Spanish Inquisition** seized a book she was writing about her beliefs. She only got it back with the help of the Spanish king.

Teresa wrote a number of books. One was called **The Way of Perfection**, published in 1565. **The Interior Castle** was published in 1567. In this book she said that a person's life is like a **castle**, and that God is like the **keeper of the castle**. By pure living and praying, a person could feel the power of God in their lives.

Protestants were not happy with Teresa's ideas. They felt they relied too much on a person's feelings and imagination. However, many people in Spain liked what she said. Her ideas promised people a closer relationship with God. Some of these people might have turned to Protestant ideas if it had not been for Teresa. Her beliefs encouraged them to stay in the Roman Catholic Church.

John of Yepes (1500–69) thought that Teresa's ideas were right. He is often remembered by the name **John of the Cross**. He was a preacher in a part of Spain called **Andalusia**. Like Teresa, John believed that a person could have a personal experience of the power of God. He made contact with mystics who were **Muslims**. He thought they might know something about God which he could learn from. Like Teresa, he was not popular with some of the powerful leaders of the Spanish Church. In 1577 he was imprisoned for one year.

During the 16th century, many Roman Catholics became more interested in miracles and experiences of God. Some historians think that the Reformation made many Roman Catholics want more out of their religion and their Church, even though they still stayed loyal to the Pope.

D **SOURCE**

- Bodies which did not rot.
- Bones which healed.
- Nuns who floated in the air.
- Hearts which caught fire.

Some of the miracles accepted in the 16th-century Roman Catholic Church.

Activities...

1 a Using your own words, explain what a **mystic** is.
  b Teresa's books were seized by the Inquisition. Does this mean that her ideas were the same as those of Protestants?
  c Read Sources C and D. Why might some 16th-century Protestants not agree with these beliefs?

2 Read Source A. Does the life of Teresa seem to agree or disagree with what this historian says?

3 Source B was carved for a famous church in Rome. Source C is Teresa's own description of her vision. Imagine you are an historian studying the importance of Teresa's life. Compare the value of these two sources for your project.

C **SOURCE**

An angel appeared to me. He carried a spear tipped with fire. He plunged the spear into my heart. I was left on fire with a great love for God.

Teresa describes her vision in 1561.

6.4 The Jesuits

Some of the most dedicated opponents of 16th-century Protestant ideas were the **Jesuits**. They were members of a Roman Catholic organization whose full name was **The Society of Jesus**.

The person who set up this organization was called **Ignatius of Loyola** (1491–1556). He had been a soldier but was badly wounded in 1521. While he was recovering he felt called by God to serve Christ. He hung up his sword before the altar of the Virgin Mary at Montserrat. He spent a year praying about what he should do, at the monastery of Manresa. He wrote a book called *Spiritual Exercises.* In it he wrote about how a Roman Catholic should be obedient to God and the Pope.

At first, Ignatius planned to travel to the **Middle East** to preach about Jesus to the people who believed in **Islam**. He wanted to **convert** the Muslim world to the Roman Catholic faith. In the end this plan did not work out. Instead he formed a group of men who were willing to do whatever the Pope asked them to do. In 1540 Pope Paul III said that he agreed with this idea.

The Jesuits' speciality was total personal obedience to the Pope. They swore to own nothing and never to marry. In 1556 there were 1,500 Jesuits. By 1626 there were 15,544. Ignatius encouraged the Jesuits to preach to non-Christians. Soon, though, the Jesuits were working hard to oppose Protestant ideas. They set up schools to spread Roman Catholic ideas. They opposed Protestants in **France**, modern **Belgium**, **southern Germany** and **eastern Europe**. Some Spanish Jesuits even thought it was right to murder Protestant rulers. This kind of murder is called **assassination**. In 1584 a leading Dutch Protestant – William of Orange – was assassinated.

In 1549 the Jesuits set up a base in **Bavaria**, southern Germany. They were encouraged by **Albert**, the Roman Catholic Duke of Bavaria. He wanted to stop Bavaria becoming Protestant. The Jesuits succeeded in stopping some of the worst things that were going on in the Roman Catholic Church there. They also defended Roman Catholic beliefs. Bavaria was prevented from becoming Protestant.

SOURCE A

I will believe that the white object I see is black if that is what I am told by the Church.

A comment made by Ignatius of Loyola in the 16th century.

SOURCE B

Give me a child until he is aged 7 and he will stay a Roman Catholic all of his life.

Jesuit saying from the 16th century.

SOURCE C

Obey the Pope and the Jesuit commander as unquestioningly as a dead person.

Jesuit saying from the 16th century.

SOURCE D

Teach us good Lord to serve you as you deserve. To give and not to count the cost. To fight and not to care about wounds. To toil and not to ask for rest. To work and not to ask for any payment except knowing that we do what you want, through Jesus Christ our Lord.

Prayer of Ignatius of Loyola, 1535.

Other Jesuits went abroad to preach to non-Christians. By the early 17th century, there were Jesuits all over the world, from **Japan** to **North** and **South America**.

The Pope sent other Jesuits to countries in Europe. Their job was to persuade the rulers to stay friendly with Rome. The Roman Catholic rulers of **France**, **Poland** and **Bavaria** had personal advisors who were Jesuits. These representatives of the Pope were called **legates**. Many Protestants hated and feared the Jesuits.

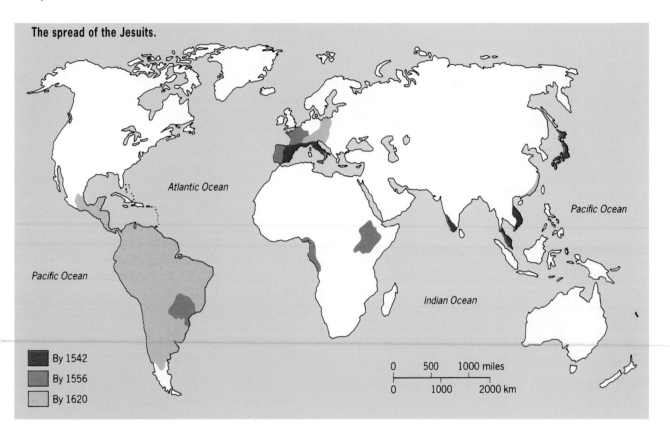

The spread of the Jesuits.

Atlantic Ocean

Pacific Ocean

Pacific Ocean

Indian Ocean

By 1542
By 1556
By 1620

0   500   1000 miles
0   1000   2000 km

Activities...

1 a List at least three things that Jesuits did to stop the spread of Protestant ideas.

   b Arrange your list in order of importance. The most important should be placed at number one. Explain how you made your decisions.

   c Read Source A. What did Ignatius mean? Explain it in your own words. How did this approach to life make the Jesuits a dangerous enemy for the Protestants?

2 'The Jesuit organization was set up to stamp out the Protestants. Their history shows this to be true.'
Do you agree or disagree with this statement? Back up your answer with evidence from this unit.

3 Read Source D. What information could this give an historian about the kind of man Ignatius of Loyola was?

6.5 Building for God

By the end of the 16th century, it was clear that the Roman Catholic Church would survive. The Counter Reformation had reorganized the Church. Roman Catholics were more confident and clear about their beliefs. They were no longer afraid that Protestants would gain control in Europe.

This confidence showed itself in magnificently decorated churches. In **Rome** the painters **Raphael** and **Michelangelo** worked on superb paintings for churches. Their work can still be seen in the **Vatican Palace** and in the church of **St Peter**. The painter **Titian** worked in **Venice**. After about 1550 this kind of decoration increased. The artists **della Porta** and **Maderna** carried on the work in Rome. The artist **Tintoretto** continued the work in Venice.

The new churches were designed to amaze visitors. They were decorated in gold and silver. These churches were designed to make people aware of the beauty of God. They also reminded visitors of the power and wealth of the Roman Catholic Church. This type of decoration came to be called **baroque**.

Baroque churches were built in **Italy** and **Spain**. They were later also built in Roman Catholic parts of Germany, such as **Bavaria**. In the baroque churches the decorations and paintings reminded people of Roman Catholic beliefs.

Activities...

1 a Write a definition of the word **baroque**.
  b Give at least two different reasons for building baroque churches.

2 a Read Source A. Is this a **fact** or an **opinion**? How can you tell?
  b Imagine that you were one of the builders of a baroque church. Would you agree with the writer of Source A? Give reasons.

3 How might Source D be useful to an historian studying the Counter Reformation?

4 Compare Source D with Source D on page 57 (Unit 7.2).
  a In what ways were Roman Catholic churches different from Calvinist ones?
  b Why were they different?

5 Read Source C. What did this historian mean?

A **SOURCE**

A visitor to them [baroque churches] will often find the dead body of a saint exposed on or under the altar. Death seems to be at the centre. The rich and powerful Church, rather than Christ, is at the centre.

From 'The History of Christianity' by R. Linder, 1990.

B **SOURCE**

The experience of Roman Catholic countries shows that one could leave the Middle Ages by several routes, of which the Reformation was only one.

From 'The European Reformation' by E. Cameron, 1991.

C **SOURCE**

While Calvinists stripped their chapels to bare essentials, baroque churches, filled with art, proclaimed the power of the Church of Rome.

From an article in 'National Geographic' by M. Severy, 1983.

The inside of the baroque church at Odenwald, Germany, built in the early 17th century.

7.1 Reformation in the Netherlands

The modern countries of the Netherlands and Belgium, known then as the Low Countries, were ruled by the King of Spain in the 16th century. In the time of Charles V, the King of Spain was also the Holy Roman Emperor and a Roman Catholic.

In the Low Countries many people wanted to be free from Spanish control. Many of these people became Protestants. As early as 1523, Lutherans in the Low Countries were being killed because of their beliefs.

In 1555 Philip II, Charles V's son, became King of Spain. He used the Inquisition to attack those Protestants who opposed him. From 1566 communities of Protestants met openly, protected by armed guards. In 1565 a large group of noblemen met together to oppose the Spanish. They made an agreement called the **Compromise of Breda**. That year, revolts began against Spanish rule. Roman Catholic churches were attacked. Many Dutch merchants were also unhappy at having to pay large taxes to the Spanish.

In 1567 the **Duke of Alva** was sent to run the Low Countries for the Spanish king. The Duke killed many thousands of Protestants. On land, the Spanish soldiers – **tercios** – were hard to beat. At sea, though, the rebels were much stronger. They were helped by the English. The Spanish soldiers took terrible revenge on the towns which had opposed them. In 1576 the town of **Antwerp** was looted. This was known as **'The Spanish Fury'**. Soon even more areas of the Netherlands were in revolt. In the area of **Brabant** even Roman Catholics rose up against the Spanish.

The southern Netherlands were recaptured by the Spanish. The northern parts remained free. In 1581 the north declared that it was independent of Spain. This became the **Dutch Republic**. Its first leader was **William the Silent**. He was later murdered. Some English soldiers were sent to help the Dutch. The Spanish were now involved in a civil war in **France**. Also their planned invasion of England (the **Armada**) had failed in 1588. The Spanish were no longer strong enough to crush the Dutch. A new, mostly Protestant country had been born.

A SOURCE

A Dutch sailor's badge, 1574. It reads: 'Better Turkish than Papist' (Roman Catholic).

B SOURCE

The Prince of Orange has bewitched the minds of all men. They love him and fear him and wish to have him as their lord.

A letter from the Governor of the Netherlands to the Spanish king, in 1576. He is writing about William the Silent.

C SOURCE

The introduction of the Inquisition aroused the anger of a stubborn and proud people.

From 'Renaissance and Reformation' by V. Green, 1964.

D

SOURCE

Philip [of Spain] had a large army in the Netherlands. With this army he could control most of the country, except for the low-lying part criss-crossed with dykes. Here the rebels kept up a resistance. They often used English ports as a refuge.

From 'Past into Present' by M. Carter, C. Culpin and N. Kinloch, 1989.

Spanish soldiers kill Protestants in Haarlem, the Netherlands, 1567.

Activities...

1 Match the following **heads** with their **tails**. Each head is a **cause**. Each tail is a **consequence**.

Heads	Tails
Spain collected high taxes	The towns were looted.
The Inquisition was used	Merchants were not happy.
Towns revolted against Spain	It made the Dutch angry.

2 Which of the secondary sources uses evidence to suggest why the Dutch revolt succeeded? What information does it give you?

3 **a** Look at Source A. What does this tell you about how this sailor felt about (i) the Turks, (ii) the Roman Catholics?

 b In your opinion which of Sources B and E best explains why the Dutch refused to surrender to the Spanish?

E

SOURCE

7.2 Reformation in France

Protestant ideas spread to France. By 1540 there were a large number of Protestants in the country. One of their leaders was **Admiral Coligny**, an important French nobleman. These French Protestants were called **Huguenots**.

France became divided. Many nobles, merchants and some workers in the towns supported the new ideas. In the countryside, though, most peasants still supported the Roman Catholic Church. In 1561 the French government complained to the Calvinist Church in Geneva. This Church had been encouraging Protestants in France.

Some French noblemen supported the Protestants as a way of getting at the Roman Catholic King of France. They were called '**political Huguenots**'. From 1559 the reigning king was a child – Charles IX. This meant that the country did not have a strong government. The political Huguenots wanted power.

In 1562 a **civil war** broke out. In the town of **Toulouse**, 3,000 Huguenots were murdered by Roman Catholics. In other towns Huguenots wrecked Roman Catholic churches. The leader of the French Roman Catholics was the **Duke of Guise**. He was murdered in 1563. For almost 30 years France was torn apart by the civil war.

In 1589 Henry IV became king. He was a Protestant. The French Roman Catholics asked for help from Roman Catholic Spain. It looked as if the civil war would get worse. In 1593 Henry changed his religion and became a Roman Catholic. Most Huguenots were horrified. Henry said he did it for peace. He promised to reform the Roman Catholic Church. In 1598 Henry published the **Edict of Nantes**. In this he promised that both Roman Catholics and Protestants had the right to live peacefully in France.

The Huguenots had the right to have their own schools and law courts. They were even allowed to keep some fortresses to protect themselves. The Edict of Nantes was very important. It offered a chance for different religious groups to live together in the same country.

A SOURCE

But for the war, France would now be Huguenot, because the people were rapidly changing their faith. But when they [the Huguenots] passed from words to weapons and began to rob, destroy and kill, the people began to say: 'What kind of religion is this?'

An extract from a report by the Ambassador of Venice, 1569.

B SOURCE

It's worth going to a Roman Catholic mass to get control of Paris.

*Henry IV is reported to have said this in 1593. (A **mass** is a Roman Catholic service.)*

C SOURCE

I am entering the Church not to live in it but to clean it.

Henry IV speaking to worried Huguenots in 1593.

The painting is by Jean Perrissin, 1565, and shows the inside of the Huguenot church at Lyons in southern France. It was called the Lyons Temple. The preacher wears a hat and his talk is timed using an hourglass.

D

E

It is the lot of the Church of God to endure blows and not to strike them. But remember, it is an anvil which has worn out many hammers.

Theodore Beza, one of the leaders of the Church at Geneva and an advisor to French Huguenots, speaking in 1562.

Activities...

1 a Suggest three reasons why Protestant ideas did not win over the Church in France.

b In your opinion which was the most important of these reasons? Explain your answer.

2 a What did Theodore Beza mean in Source E?

b Does Source A suggest that the Huguenots listened to Beza's advice, or ignored it? Explain how you reached your decision.

3 Using Source D as evidence, describe what it would have been like to attend a service in the Lyons Temple.

4 Why would many Huguenots have been shocked by what Henry is supposed to have said in Source B?

7.3 The Massacre of St Bartholomew's Day

On the night of August 23 1572, over 3,000 **Huguenots** were murdered in Paris by Roman Catholics. This is known as the **Massacre of St Batholomew's Day**. Why did this massacre take place? How did people react to what happened?

Between 1562 and 1570 there was fighting in France between Protestants and Roman Catholics (see Unit 7.2). King Charles IX of France was only a child and his mother **Queen Catherine** worked hard to stop the king being controlled by either the extreme Protestants or the extreme Catholics.

In 1572 Queen Catherine was very worried. The Protestant leader **Coligny** had become popular with the king. Coligny wanted France to attack the Spanish in the Netherlands. The queen thought that this would be a disaster for France. Coligny also encouraged disagreements between King Charles and his brothers. This angered the queen who wished to get rid of Coligny.

Those who organized the Massacre of St Bartholomew's Day acted in a panic. Instead of destroying the Huguenots, the massacre was the start of a fourth war.

From 'A History of Europe', by H. Fisher, 1935.

A late 16th-century Protestant picture of the massacre.

SOURCE

An early 19th-century picture showing the murder of Coligny.

Queen Catherine was afraid that if the king became too friendly with the Huguenots he might be overthrown by the extreme Catholic nobles who hated the Protestants. The queen and her children were Catholics but feared these nobles.

The French Huguenots and some later historians have argued that Queen Catherine planned to kill the Protestant leaders long before it happened. She may have hoped that the extreme Protestants and extreme Catholics would destroy each other and leave her in peace.

Other historians have argued that in fact Catherine did not intend it to happen this way. They think that the whole situation got out of control. On August 22 the Huguenot leader Coligny was shot. There is evidence that the queen encouraged this. She was frightened by Coligny's influence over the king. However, Coligny was only wounded. Many Huguenots were in Paris at the time and were very angry about this. It may be that the queen panicked. She struck at them before they could act. Extreme Catholics were encouraged to kill leading Huguenots, including Coligny. This turned into a terrible massacre and spread to many French cities. Thousands of innocent Huguenots were murdered. Protestants everywhere were shocked. However, **Pope Gregory XIII** was delighted, as was the Catholic King of Spain.

D

SOURCE

Catherine, fearful for her own safety between the two groups [Huguenots and extreme Catholics], decided on the awful step of trying to wipe out one of them.

From 'The Early Modern World', by C. Strong, 1968.

E

SOURCE

It is best seen as an act of desperation by a clever woman who had momentarily lost her head. But would she have hit on such a solution if it had not already been discussed by her friends?

From 'Europe Divided', by J. Elliott, 1968.

Activities...

1 Give three reasons why Queen Catherine wanted to get rid of Coligny. Which was most important?

2 Read Sources B, D and E. Which gives the impression that Catherine had not really planned the killing? Which suggests that there might have been some planning behind it ?

3 a How useful would Source C be as evidence for what happened to Coligny?
 b Why might Protestants have drawn Sources A and C?

7.4 Europe Divided

The Reformation has often been blamed for dividing Europe. The Reformation split the Christian Church. The countries of Europe had to take sides. Before the Reformation, people felt that they were part of **Christendom**. After the Reformation, they thought of themselves as Protestants or Roman Catholics. Many Protestants could not agree among themselves. Calvinists disagreed with Lutherans. Both disagreed with the Anabaptists.

There was fighting between the Roman Catholics and Protestants in the 1540s and 1550s. It only ended when both sides admitted that Germany could not be united over religion again. In the 17th century, there were even more terrible wars.

The Counter Reformation tried to stop the spread of the new ideas. In some areas it was successful. **Bavaria**, **Poland**, **Austria**, **France**, **Belgium** and **Bohemia** were stopped from becoming Protestant. Many Protestants were killed or expelled. In countries such as Spain and Italy, the Roman Catholic Church became better organized than ever before.

It is wrong, though, to think that Europe was split only between Protestants and Roman Catholics. Many old quarrels and rivalries between nations carried on, as they had before the Reformation. The **Spanish** fought in every big European war between 1500 and 1659. They fought the Protestant Dutch for 80 years and the Roman Catholic French for 50 years. In the 16th century, the **French** were happy to help the German Protestants. They did this to make problems for their enemy, the King of Spain. At times, the King of France was an ally of the Protestants in Germany and the Turkish members of the Islamic religion.

Europe was divided between the north and the south. In the north, several countries became Protestant. In the south, they stayed Roman Catholic. In the north, countries such as England and the Dutch Republic began to develop **Atlantic** trade and to expand their **economies**. The economies of Spain and Italy had stopped growing. These differences were beginning to happen before the Reformation. Some historians think that the Reformation added to a split that was happening anyway.

This was a split between **middle class** merchants and craftspeople and **peasant** farmers who lived on land owned by rich people called **aristocrats**.

A SOURCE

The Protestant problem usually had to take a back burner to crises in Italy, or Spain, or to the Turkish threat.

Professor H. Rabe, 1983, talking about why the Emperor Charles V did not crush the Protestants.

B SOURCE

At the heart of Muslim and Christian weakness was their own political disunity.

From 'The Struggle for World Power' by W. Woodruff, 1981.

C SOURCE

The leaders of the Protestant Reformation usually came from the middle classes but those of the Roman Catholic Reformation were aristocrats.

From 'Christianity Through the Centuries' by E. Cairns, 1981.

Europe in 1610, showing the religious divisions nearly 100 years after the Reformation started.

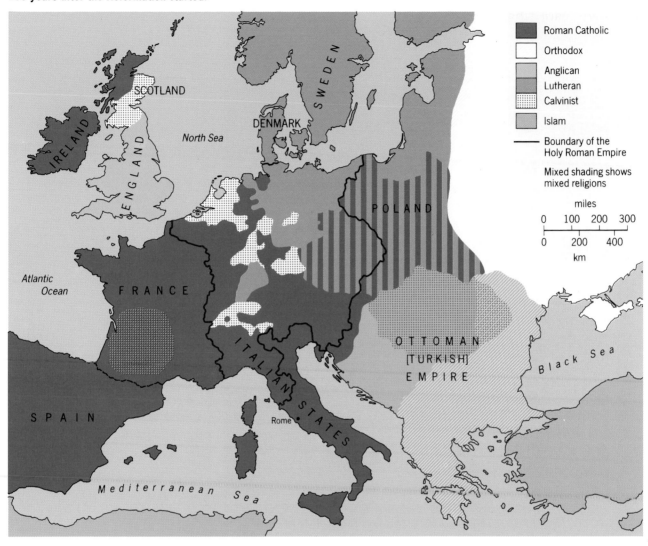

Legend:
- Roman Catholic
- Orthodox
- Anglican
- Lutheran
- Calvinist
- Islam
- Boundary of the Holy Roman Empire
- Mixed shading shows mixed religions

miles
0   100   200   300
0   200   400
km

SCOTLAND · IRELAND · ENGLAND · SWEDEN · DENMARK · North Sea · POLAND · FRANCE · ITALIAN STATES · Rome · SPAIN · Atlantic Ocean · OTTOMAN [TURKISH] EMPIRE · Black Sea · Mediterranean Sea

SOURCE D

In 1571 the Turks captured the island of Cyprus from the Venetians. This led to the formation of a Christian league which annihilated the Turkish fleet in the great battle of Lepanto.

From 'Pursuit of Power' by J. Davis, 1970.

Activities...

1 a Why might people think that the Reformation split Europe?
   b Why is it important evidence that Spain fought the French **and** the Dutch in the 16th century?

2 a What evidence is there that Christian countries could work together if they felt they were under threat?
   b Which source suggests that countries being unable to agree was not necessarily the fault of the Christian Reformation?

3 In the 1520s the Pope accused Luther's ideas of being responsible for 'division, war, murder and the collapse of Christendom'. Using the evidence in this unit say what you think.

A

SOURCE

Jesus as painted by the Dutch painter Rembrandt, 1606–69. It shows Jesus looking like a real Jewish man. Before this, most painters had made him look like a European with a halo.

B

SOURCE

O God, if Luther is dead who will explain to us the Gospel [the Good News about Jesus].

A comment made by the German artist Albrecht Dürer, 1521.

C

SOURCE

You should read Luther to know whether he is right or wrong. We read everything.

Roman Catholic monk at the German monastery of Munnerstadt, 1983.

The ideas of the Reformation changed history. The Roman Catholic Church was no longer the one Church in Europe. People who became Protestants believed they would only get to heaven if they sincerely believed in God. They did not need to rely on a priest or the Pope. This made what individuals thought and did much more important.

Many rulers were glad to become free of the power of the Pope. Some German rulers used Protestant ideas as an excuse for rebelling against the Roman Catholic Holy Roman Empire. People began to read the Bible and worship God in their own language. Soon, more and more books were being written in modern languages. In Germany the language of the new Bible helped people to decide on what was 'proper' German. There was also better education.

The Roman Catholic Church changed, too. The **Counter Reformation** made the Church better organized and more confident. Roman Catholics, like the **Jesuits**, carried Roman Catholic beliefs to thousands of people in **Asia**, **Africa** and **South America**. Many of these countries are still Roman Catholic today.

In many Protestant countries, ideas about art changed. Paintings and drawings became much more lifelike. They carried the message that God was interested in every aspect of life and the world. Artists like **Dürer** in the 16th century and **Rembrandt** in the 17th century were influenced by Protestant ideas.

Some historians feel that because Luther opposed the revolutionary Protestants he helped to make the ruling princes stronger than ever. In Germany the Lutheran Church did what it was told by the rulers. The beliefs of poorer people, like the Anabaptists, were crushed. This happened in many Protestant countries. The ideas of the Reformation often had least support among the **peasants**.

Some of the effects of the Reformation.

The Pope lost authority over many rulers.

The Church was split.

The rulers were more powerful.

For many people, what was most important was what an individual believed.

Many Protestants disagreed with each other. They would not listen to each other's ideas.

Activities...

1 a Read Source B. According to Dürer, why was Luther so important?

b Make a list of the other ways in which the Reformation ideas changed people's lives.

c Arrange your list in order of importance. How did you decide?

2 Imagine you are choosing one of three books written on the Reformation by a Protestant, a Roman Catholic, and a Muslim. What **might** be the strengths and weaknesses of each?

3 a How might Source C be used to show how ideas can change over time?

b How could an historian use Source A as a way of showing the influence of Reformation ideas?

Africa 4
Alexander VI, Pope 16, 17
Anabaptists 32, 33, 34, 35, 36, 37, 63
Armada 54
artists 52, 61, 63
Augsburg, Confession of 30
Augsburg, Diet of 24
Augsburg, Peace of 25
Augustinians 19
Austria 60
Ávila, Teresa of 48, 49

baroque 52, 53
Bavaria 50, 51, 52, 60
Belgium 4, 50, 54, 60
Beza, Theodore 57
Bible translation 10, 13, 14, 21, 31, 62
Böhm, Hans 29
Borgia, Rodrigo 16, 17
Breda, Compromise of 54
Brethren of the Common Life 15
Brüderhof 37
Bullinger, Heinrich 39
Bundschuh 29

Cabot, John 4
Cajetan, Cardinal 19
Cajob, Jorg 37
Calvin, John 40, 42, 43
Caraffa, Cardinal 47
Carmelite Order of nuns 48
Catherine, Queen of France 58, 59
chantry priests 7
Charles V, King of Spain and Holy
    Roman Emperor 4, 8, 20, 21, 23, 24,
    25, 54
Charles IX, King of France 56, 58
Christendom 6
Clement VII, Pope 45
Coligny, Admiral 56, 58, 59
Columbus, Christopher 4
communion 23, 31, 39, 43
consistory 31, 42
Contarini, Gasparo 44
Czechoslovakia 32, 37

della Porta 52
Denmark 26
devotio moderna 15
Diaz, Bartholomew 4
Dominicans 19, 46
Dürer, Albrecht 11, 14, 63

education 10, 13, 15, 16, 18, 41, 42, 50,
    56, 62
Edward VI, King of England 26
Elizabeth I, Queen of England 26
England 4, 8, 14, 26, 54, 60
Erasmus 10, 11, 13, 23, 39
exploration 4

Farel, Guillaume 41
Ferdinand, King of Spain 8
feudal system 28
Forest Cantons 39
France 4, 9, 25, 26, 43, 47, 50, 51, 54,
    56, 57, 58, 60
Frederick, Elector of Saxony 20, 22

Gama, Vasco da 4
Geneva Academy 41
Germany 8, 13, 14, 15, 17, 18, 20, 25,
    26, 28, 29, 30, 32, 37, 50, 52, 53, 61

Godly princes 30
Grebel, Conrad 32
Greece 6
Greek 10
Gregory XIII, Pope 59
Groote, Geert 15
Gutenberg, Johann 13
'Gutenberg' Bible 13

Henry II, King of France 25, 47
Henry IV, King of France 56
Henry VII, King of England 8
Henry VIII, King of England 8, 26
heretics 13, 46
Holy Roman Empire 4, 20, 45
Hubmaier, Balthasar 32
Huguenots 56, 57, 58, 59
Humanists 10
Hungary 26
Hutter, Jakob 37
Hutterites 37
hymns 31

incunabula 13
Index 47
indulgences 18, 45
Inquisition 46, 47, 49
Isabella, Queen of Spain 8
Islam 4, 5, 24, 25, 37, 49, 50, 54, 60, 61
Italy 4, 45, 47, 52, 60

John of the Cross 49
Julius II, Pope 6
Justification by Faith 31

Kappel, Battle of 39
Karlstadt, Andreas 22
Kempis, Thomas à 15
Knox, John 26, 41

Lateran Council 17
legates 51
Leo X, Pope 17, 23, 44
Lepanto, Battle of 61
Leyden, Jan of 34, 35
Lollards 14
Loyola, Ignatius of 50
Luther, Martin 18, 19, 20, 21, 22, 23,
    25, 26, 28, 29, 30, 31, 32, 33, 38, 40,
    41, 46, 63
Lutherans 26

Maderna 52
Mainz, Archbishop 18
marriage 16, 31, 35, 39
Martin V, Pope 10
Mary, Queen of Scots 26
Matthys, Jan 34
Maurice, Prince of Saxony 25
Melanchthon, Philip 22
Mennonites 36, 37
Meyer, Anna 39
Michelangelo 52
Muhammad II, Sultan 5
Mühlberg, Battle of 25
Münster 34, 35
Müntzer, Thomas 29, 33
mystics 48

Nantes, Edict of 56
Netherlands 4, 8, 10, 15, 25, 26, 34, 36,
    37, 54, 55, 60
New Testament 10, 30

North America 4
Norway 26
nuncios 8

Oratory of Divine Love 44
Order of St Francis 14
Orthodox Church 6
Ottoman Empire 4

papacy 4, 6, 8, 16, 17, 18, 20, 30, 49, 61
Papal States 4
Passau, Treaty of 25
patriotism 8
Paul III, Pope 45, 50
Paul IV, Pope 47
Peasants' War 23, 28, 29, 33
Philip II, King of Spain 54, 55
pilgrimage 18
Poland 4, 26, 27, 51, 60
Poliziano, Angelo 10
preaching 31
predestination 40
purgatory 18

radical reformers 22, 23, 32, 33, 34, 35,
    36, 37
Raphael 52
Regensburg, Diet of 25
Rembrandt 63
Renaissance 10, 11
Russia 6
Russian Empire 4

St Bartholomew's Day, Massacre of 58
Sattler, Michael 32
Saxony 17, 20, 24, 25, 31
Schmalkald League 24
Scotland 4, 8, 26
Simmons, Menno 36
Society of Jesus 50, 51, 63
South America 4
Spain 4, 6, 8, 45, 46, 47, 48, 49, 52, 54,
    55, 60
Spanish Fury 54
Speyer, Diet of 23
Storch, Nicholas 22, 33
Stübner, Markus 22
Sweden 26
Switzerland 8, 15, 26, 32, 38, 40

Tetzel, Johann 18, 19
Thirty Years War 37
Tintoretto 52
Titian 52
trade 8, 17, 28, 33, 34, 37, 60
Trent, Council of 44, 45
Turkey 4

Venice 8

wars of religion 25, 39, 56, 58
Wartburg Castle 21, 22, 23
Wessel, John of 14
William the Silent 54
William of Orange 50
Worms, Diet of 20, 21
Wyclif, John 14

Zwickau Prophets 22
Zwingli, Huldreich 23, 38, 40